The Wax Persona

by Yury Tynyanov

*Translated and with notes on
the text and the author
by Colin Bearne*

*Illustrations by Amanda Goldsmith
Production by Jaki Porter*

© Colin Bearne February 2017

Contents

Yury Tynyanov - Biographical Note

Yury Tynyanov was born in 1894 in the little town of Rezhitsa, now Rezekne in modern day Latvia, but then part of the Russian Empire. As he points out himself in his autobiography, the town was only some six hours away from the birthplaces of Mihoels, Chagall, and Catherine I. If we allow for modern travel facilities the journeys between these places are much shortened.

Even in 1894 the little town was a very melting-pot of nationalities and remote from the elegant and cultured atmosphere of the large cities surrounding it from three sides. It is no wonder that the young Yury became filled with a deep interest in history and historical figures.

His father was a much-respected doctor in the town, but his family lived not in the commercial centre but on the high road with its varied passing traffic. Yury spent much of his time outside in the garden, or on the bridge on the highroad where the beggars sat. The boy's interests were even then out of the ordinary, taking in the eccentrics and feeble-minded who roamed the streets. He also spent time in the vicinity of one of the most substantial buildings in the town – the prison.

The written word and the moving image came early into his life – at seven he watched his first film show – and by eight he was already reading newspapers. His father's literary tastes took in Saltykov-Shchedrin and Gorky, and Yury also came to them early. Significantly for his later writing, he was given a collection of Pushkin for his eighth birthday. It is interesting to note that it was the lesser known byways of the poet's writings that attracted and amused him.

When Yury was 9 he went to the gymnasium in Pskov, and over the next few years the place became his second home. Here he continued reading, and, like most boys of his age, spent his spare money on comic books and adventure stories. Visits to the circus

gave stimulus to an already developing penchant for the eccentric and the grotesque. His school years are strangely coloured by the number of his colleagues who were driven to commit suicide. Death seems to play a major part in this writer's own narrative of his youth. He also witnessed the after-effects of the abortive uprising of 1905. The punitive backlash was felt particularly harshly by the student community.

In 1912 Tynyanov went to St Petersburg University where he joined the Russian and Slavonic Department in the Faculty of History and Philology. He became immersed in the study of Pushkin and Griboyedov. The choice of department reflected his fascination with words and history. As he himself puts it: "If I had not had the childhood I had – I would never have understood history." And he goes on to say, "If there had been no revolution – I would never have understood literature." The first post-revolutionary year, 1918, found Tynanov in fact seriously ill with a bout of the illness which would eventually prove fatal. It was the writer's fascination with how literature, particularly Pushkin, which led to him joining OPOYAZ[01] and becoming acquainted with leading figures in the Formalist Movement. He remained a member of the group until its eventual dissolution. The group brought him into contact with literary activists such as Kaverin, Shklovsky, Eichenbaum and Chukovsky. He was never a leading light in the circle, but despite his somewhat introverted personality, his wit and perspicacity impressed all who met him. His best known works all appeared during this period, regardless of the fact that the encroaching MS rendered him bedridden and housebound for long periods.

Like many of his contemporaries he was intrigued by the cinema, films and the teamwork and interplay of talents involved in making them. This cannot but have influenced his prose writings, in particular the historical 'docufiction' of Kyukhlya, *The Death of Vazir Mukhtar*, *Pushkin*, *The Young Vitushishnikov* and also Voskovaya persona – *The Wax Persona*. In fact shortly before Tynyanov's death

[01] *The Society for the Study of Poetic Language*

in hospital in 1943 Sergei Eisenstein had been about to propose collaboration on a film.

There were two occasions on which Tynyanov's manuscripts and papers were lost or destroyed, at the time of the Revolution and during the onset of the purges in the late 1930s. This has meant that many originals have disappeared, especially originals of the theoretical writings. Since the end of the Soviet Union these have been more widely discussed and republished, but, with the exception of one or two texts, less attention has been paid to the prose fiction. Even less has been devoted to Voskovaya persona, and it is hoped that the present translation will bring the work to a wider audience.

Notes on the text

Tynyanov's longer prose fiction works are relatively well-known, and have been translated into English, as have some of the theoretical writings. Voskovaya persona has been appreciated in the original language, but given little prominence in critical works. The novella/story is in the Russian tradition, however, with its atmospheric echoes of Gogol' and Dostoyevsky. It is difficult to find an appopriate genre label - though Kaverin's assessment that it is a work of "docufiction" helps to make it more approachable by the twenty-first century reader, to whom this kind of writing is familiar, and its debt to Charles Dickens and Maksim Gorky in the Fortuna Tavern scenes and the portrayal of the shadowy crook figure is obvious.

The *Wax Persona* obstinately shrugs off the application of most generic labels. It is neither tale (rasskaz), nor novella (povest), nor novel (roman), yet it has traces of the literary procedures to be encountered in all these. There are also stumbling blocks to 'normal' reading. The narrative is only loosely sequential, and contains archaisms of both specifically historical and colloquial origin. Victor Shklovsky, critic and colleague of Tynyanov, describes the structure of *The Wax Persona* as 'the unfolding of a metaphor'. In addition the narrative is strangely episodic and incomplete. Interwoven in the text are sequences of 'stream of consciousness' techniques; for example the episode of the contents of the Dutch stove tiles. Both the tiles and the narrative itself exhibit some of the techniques of ornamentalism.

At times the narrator – a somewhat puzzling presence – seems to have taken on the role of a camera. Film techniques abound in the status awarded objects and symbols. For example, the hands and fingers of some of the leading characters, their postures and gestures. Because of the cumulative effect of the factors already mentioned it becomes very difficult to identify a 'hero'. It ought to be Peter. In a 'normal' sequential narrative it might have been, but not in this one.

Instead there are rivals for our attention, the 'monster' Yakov and his 'soldier' brother. There is the pair of competing 'courtiers' Menshikov and Yaguzhinsky, typical of the non-noble families with whom Peter had surrounded himself. Then there is the pathetic nymphomaniac tsarina, Catherine. The only thread of continuity might seem to be the foreign artist and architect, Rastrelli, a survivor amidst the internecine strife. We learn more about these figures than we are told about Peter himself. It nevertheless remains a perceptive interpretation of the Russia of Peter the Great, exploring both its positive and its negative sides. It reflects the miasmic and impermanent nature of Peter's city – a city which functioned, when it did, by virtue of a strange mixture of fear, cruelty, rivalry and betrayal. Yakov's deformity is masked, as are so many other emotional deformities, by 'normal' outward appearances, in his case by the acquisition of a pair of mittens. This is deception in a narrative where deception is a most powerful motive force.

Kaverin was not the only critic to note the parallels with Stalin's Russia. Had Tynyanov not died of illness when he did he would almost inevitably have suffered in one of the wartime o post-war purges.

As for the wax effigy of the title, created during the course of a lengthy and often interrupted narrative, it is assembled not by any Russian, but by the foreign artist Rastrelli, patronised by Peter before his death, and by subsequent tsars and tsarinas. We should also note the irony of the fact that this very lifelike waxwork should finally come to rest as an exhibit in the building housing the collection of sometimes macabre 'curiosities' that Peter himself had assembled. In the meantime a former 'curiosity', Yakov the six fingered one, gains his freedom.

Peter's effigy is even more lifelike, however, in that it moves. Lifelike automata had been fashionable in Europe before Peter's time. There are records from the 1660s of a pair of mechanical lions as part of the décor in one of the palaces of the Moscow Kremlin. The lions could be made to open their mouths and roar. It is interesting to note in this respect that the movements made by Peter's effigy were interpreted by his courtiers not as signs of welcome but as wrathful commands – a finger of accusation pointing at them. Thus is emphasis given to the system of fear, accusation and counter-accusation which formed the dynamic of Peter' 'court'. The parallels with Stalin's Russia are there for all who wish to see them, and there is a particularly piquant moment in the classic TV docudrama "Red Monarch" when Beria, mocking the dead leader's corpse, suddenly starts back in horror when one of Stalin's eyes slowly opens and closes.

The Wax Persona

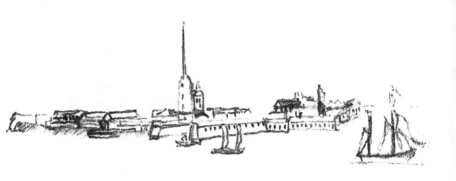

Chapter One

"Oh, faithful doctor, deign to cure me
Remove my painful wound"
Entry on the calendar.

1

As recently as Thursday there had been drinking. And what drinking it was! But now he was screaming day and night until he was hoarse.

Now he was dying.

What drinking on Thursday! But now his personal physician, Blumentrost, held out little hope for him. On Thursday they had put Yakov Turgenev arse-first into a wash-tub, and in the wash-tub there were eggs. But it hadn't really been fun. Somehow it had been awkward, for Turgenev was a simple old man. He had clucked like a hen, and then burst into tears – it had been hard for him.

The canals had not been dug. The Neva towpath was in a mess. His orders had not been carried out. And had he really got to be dying now, in the midst of all these unfinished projects?

His sister would not see him: she was cunning and wicked. The nun could not bear him. She was stupid. His son hated him. He was stubborn. Danilovich, his favourite and right-hand man, was a thief. And it had come to light that Vilim Ivanovich had been muttering angrily to his lady that there was too much drinking going on, and

3

that there was one outstanding toper, not just anyone, but his Master.

He was lying cocooned in his bed, wrapped in bedding up to the very fabric covered ceiling. The bed was beginning to move about like a boat. This was the convulsions caused by his illness, but he was also shivering himself, on purpose.

Yekaterina was bending over him with what she had brought him for his soul, for meat – her breasts. Those breasts which only two months previously were being kissed by the Honourable Chamberlain – Mons, Vilim Ivanovich.

He lay still.

In the neighbouring chamber the Italian doctor, Lazaretti, short, dark-skinned and wiry, was warming his hands, and that English doctor, Horn, was sharpening a long knife with which to bleed him.

They had put Mons's head in spirit, and it was now standing in its jar in the Kunstkammer[02] - for scientific study.

To whom was he to leave this great Science, the whole superstructure, the State, and finally a not inconsiderable art collection?

Oh, Katya, Katya, rude, coarse woman!

2

Danilych, Prince of Izhorsk, had not bothered to undress. He was sitting in his bedchamber and dozing – would they be coming for him?

For so long now he had schooled himself to sit for a while and doze and ponder: he expected imminent punishment for his plundering of the monasteries, for his false survey in the Pochepsk district and the huge bribes he had been given. Some had given him a hundred

---

[02]Chamber of curiosities (German), building housing Peter's collection of art objects and objects of curiosity

thousand each, and some fifty silver thalers each, from the towns and from the peasantry, from foreigners of various ranks and standing, and from the Imperial court, and then there was the signing of contracts in a false name, the claims for clothing the troops, the mock preparation of unsuitable harbours – and all this paid for direct by the Exchequer. His nose was red and pointed, and his hands were dry. He liked everything to come alight in his hands. He wished everything to be of the best quality and in plentiful supply, wanted everything to be neat and tidy.

In the evenings he would reckon up his profit and loss.

Vassilevsky Island was gifted to me and almost at once taken away again. In the last round of grants to the army I was passed over, and the only great comfort to me will be if I am given the town of Baturin.

His Highness Prince Danilych would normally summon his minister, Volkov, and ask him to report on how many properties he currently owned. Then he would shut himself away while he still had the last figure fresh in his mind, fifty two thousand subject serfs, or he would recall the livestock and salt undertakings he had in Archangel town – and he would feel a sort of secret sense of enjoyment round his lips, a sort of sensuous pleasure from all his possession, from the fact that he had a lot of everything, more than anyone else, and that it was all increasing. He was building up the army, building with speed and assiduity, he was a diligent and willing master, he had avoided military action, and was finishing the construction of the canals, and his hands were still dry and burning. They needed work, or a woman, or a bribe.

Danilych, Prince of Rome, loved a bribe. Already he could not take in with one single glance all his possessions, how many towns, villages and serfs were his. Sometimes he even said to himself with some surprise: "The more I control, the more my fingers itch for more."

He would sometimes wake up at night, in his deep alcove bed, and would look at his wife, Mikhailovna, Princess of Izhorsk, and he would give a sigh: "You stupid woman, you!"

Then, turning his burning gaze to the window, to the Asiatic glass panes, or staring at the ceilings decorated with leather, he would calculate how much interest he would get from the Exchequer, so that in the accounting he could show less, but in fact receive more grain. And he worked out sometimes a thousand for five hundred silver thalers, and sometimes six hundred and fifty for everything.

Then a feeling of weak vulnerability would come over him.

Then,once more, he would cast a long hard stare at Mikhailovna: "Blubber lips!".

And then he would deftly and quickly thrust his feet into his Tartar slippers, and go into the adjoining chamber, belonging to his sister-in-law, Varvara. The latter understood him better, and he would talk with her of this and that, sometimes until the very morning. And he enjoyed it. Some of the old fools said he should not do it – that it was a sin. But, after all, the room was only next door, and there was nothing stopping him. His action even encouraged him to feel a certain boldness of status.

But, at the same time, he was fond of a small bribe, and would sometimes as a result, say to his sister-in-law Varvara, or to Mikhailovna herself, Countess of Pochep: "How can I enjoy all my possessions when I cannot see them all at once or even comprehend them all? I have seen ten thousand men in formation or in an encampment – a swarm of a whole ten thousand – and according to Minister Volkov's information, I have fifty two thousand souls, not counting beggars and elderly do-nothings. You just can't take all that in, and yet a bribe is there in my hand, grasped by my five fingers as though it were a living thing!

And now, after the process of many bribes, large and small, and much plundering, and the exile of all his spiteful enemies, including Baron Shafir, the Jew, and many others, he was sitting waiting punishment, and he would constantly think to himself, pursing his lips: "I'll give back half and laugh it off."

And after downing a glass of Rhenish, he would mentally enjoy thinking of one particular place, his home town, and he would add: "But Baturin – that's mine!"

But then things went from bad to worse, and it was not hard to see he might lose both nostrils[03] – exile and hard-labour. There was only one hope in such a calamitous fall from grace – a lot of his money had been transferred to London and Amsterdam – that might be useful later on.

But those born under the planet Venus – Bruce[04] had been talking-about this – would have their wishes fulfilled, and get out of trouble.

Then he too had fallen ill.

Now Danilych was sitting waiting: when would they summon him? Mikhailovna was all the time praying that it would be soon. It was now two nights that he had been sitting in the entrance hall – in full uniform. And then, when he was sitting waiting, a servant entered and announced. "Count Rastrelli, on special business!"

"What the devil has brought him here?" said the prince in amazement, "and his title is a worthless one!"

But then in came the same Count Rastrelli. His title of Count was not a real one. It was a papal one. The Pope had created him a count for something or other, either that or he had bought the title from the Pope, but all he was in reality was an "artist".

3

He had been admitted with his assistant, Monsieur Legendre. The latter had walked along the street with a lantern, lighting the way for Rastrelli, and had announced at the door that he also, the assistant Legendre, begged to be admitted because he had a more fluent command of foreign languages.

---

[03]Slitting of the nostrils was a frequently used punishment in Russia at the time.

[04]A Scot in the service of Peter's Russia

So they had both been admitted.

Rastrelli mounted the staircase energetically, his hand resting on the stair rail as though it were the handle of his cane. His hands were round and red and small in size. He did not look at anything around him, because this house had been built by the German, Schedel, and what was built by a German was of no interest to Rastrelli. Once in the study he stood still with proud humility. He was small in stature, with a large stomach and fleshy cheeks. His feet were small like a woman's, and his hands were rounded. He was leaning on his cane, out of breath, and breathing noisily and heavily through his nose.

He had a lumpy, bumpy nose, the colour of Bordeaux, like a sponge or the Dutch tufa that goes round a fountain. His nose was like a triton's. The consumption of much vodka, and the demands of his great art caused Rastrelli to breathe heavily. He loved roundness, and if he was depicting a Neptune, especially a bearded one, he was fond of surrounding it with splashing mermaids. In this way, along the banks of the Neva he had rounded off up to a hundred pieces in bronze, and all of them amusing subjects from Aesop's fables. Just opposite the Menshikov house itself (for example) there stood the bronze statue of a frog, looking as though it would puff itself up until it finally burst. The frog was so lifelike that its eyes seemed to be popping out. It would be little to give a million to such a man, once you had enticed him to work for you. He had more pleasure and artistry in his little finger than any German. On his trip from Paris to Petersburg alone he had spent ten thousand in French money. Menshikov could still not get over this. And he even felt a certain admiration for it. How much art could he alone produce? Menshikov looked in amazement at his thick calves. However painful they might be Rastrelli was obviously a strong man. But of course, as a noble, Danilych was seated in an armchair while Rastrelli was standing to talk. What he was saying in Italian and French his assistant, Legendre, understood and conveyed to the Prince of Izhorsk in Russian.

Rastrelli gave a bow and announced that the 'duc d'Izhorsk' was a fine gentleman, and a wonderful patron of the arts. He was the father of the arts, and that it was for that simple reason that he had come.

"Your Highness, father of the arts", this is how Legendre conveyed what he said, but instead of 'arts' he said 'pieces', because he knew the word 'shtuk' in Polish meant 'arts'.

At this point Minister Volkov thought that Rastrelli was talking about busts and bronze statues, but Danilovych dismissed this. Rastrelli was hardly likely to have come at such an hour to discuss bits of statuary.

And he waited.

Then Rastrelli lodged a complaint about Monsieur de Caravaque. The latter was an artist for small items. He painted people on a small scale. And he had arrived in Russia at the same time as the Count.

But the 'duc' had shown his patronly favour and begun to employ Rastrelli as an historical specialist, and given him the contract for depicting the battle of Poltava. But now the Count had heard a rumour that de Caravaque was also beginning work on this subject, and he had come to ask the 'duc' to intervene. Rastrelli distorted the name Caravaque as though he were squawking like a bird. Spittle sprayed out of his mouth as he said it. Danilych fixed his gaze on him. He was beginning to enjoy the spectacle of the artist's discomfiture. Why should not Caravaque talk about it? He was a quickwitted artist – and he charged less. The spat between Rastrelli and Caravaque amused him. And if it had not been the time it was what would he have done? He would have set up an evening and invited both Rastrelli and Caravaque. Then he would have egged them on until they came to blows. They would have been like fighting cocks – the fat one and the dark-skinned one!

Then Rastrelli said, and Legendre translated: Rumours had reached him that when the Emperor died de Caravaque wanted to make a death mask from him, and de Caravaque did not know how to do masks, but he, Rastrelli, knew how to make death masks.

At this Menshikov gave a gentle stretch in his chair, got up from it quickly and smoothly, and ran to the door. He looked behind the door and then stared for a long time out of the window. He was looking to check there were no spies or informers.

Then he advanced on Rastrelli, and said the following: "Why are you gabbling such words unacceptable to His Imperial Majesty? The Emperor is alive, and has even shown some improvement."

But at this Rastrelli shook his head vigorously: "No, the Emperor will die within four days. The doctor, Lazaretti, told me so".

And then, as though to explain what he meant, he pointed two short, fat fingers at the floor, meaning the Emperor would be buried within four days.

At this a chill shiver ran through Menshikov's body, because none of the people around him had yet spoken so frankly about the Tsar dying. He felt ecstatic, and it was as though his ecstasy had raised him off the floor, above his present state. Everything in him had changed, and now when he sat at a table, or in his armchair, he was a calm man, a patron of the arts, a man no longer interested in any insignificant bribes.

Rastrelli then said, and the assistant and Minister Volkov interpreted, each in his own way: "He, Rastrelli, wanted to do the mask, since he hoped such an intriguing object would attract considerable attention at foreign courts, both with the Kaiser, and in France. In addition he, Rastrelli, promised to take a mask from the Prince himself when he died, and he was also willing to do a portrait, small, and in bronze, of the prince's daughter".

"You tell him", said Danilych, "I'll be the one that takes a mask from him and he also is to make a medium size of my daughter. The fool."

And Rastrelli said he would.

But then, stamping his foot and pursing his lips, he suddenly stuck out his right arm – his right hand sparkled with rubies and garnets – and began to speak so quickly, that Legendre and Volkov could not interpret, and stood with their mouths gaping open. What he said was like bubbles, which suddenly float around someone when they are swimming, and just as quickly burst. The bubbles rose up and then burst - and finally the man swimming dived back under. Count Rastrelli choked to a stop. It was all then translated to the prince. There is the kind of portrait which is splendid and of the most faithful kind, so that it is impossible to tell the portrait apart from the subject. Neither bronze, nor brass, nor the softest of leads, nor gesso can compete with portraits done by an artist in this medium. Art in this medium is one of the oldest and longest lived forms. It even goes back to the times of the Roman emperors. This medium jumps into your hand all of its own, it is so pliable. The slightest hollow or bump – it will convey them all. You only have to press it or spread it out with the palm of your hand, or model with your fingers, or work it with a stylos, and then shape it, smooth it, then work it with your palm, even it out – and what emerges? A masterpiece!

Menshikov watched uneasily as Rastrelli gestured, modelling the imaginary substance with his fingers. The fingers modelling were small, misshapen by the cold and vodka, red and wrinkled. And finally something else came to light: some two hundred or so years ago the figure of a girl had been unearthed, buried in the soil of Italy. Everything about the figure was entirely lifelike, both from the front and from the back. Some said the statue was the work of the master Raphael. Others said it was by Andrea Verrochio or Orsini.

At this point Rastrelli suddenly burst out laughing like a very young child. His eyes disappeared, his nose wrinkled up, and he exclaimed, stamping his foot: "But it was Julia, daughter of the famous Cicero – alive! Not actually alive, that is, but with the passage of time Nature itself had made the figure look like that".

And Rastrelli gave a choking gasp and said: "and this figure was made of – Wax!"

"How much do they want for this girl?" asked the Prince

"She's not for sale," said Legendre

"She's not for sale", said Volkov

"Well, there's no point talking about her then", said the Prince.

But at this Rastrelli lifted his small, fat arm. "You tell the duc d'Izhorsk" he commanded, "that lifesize wax portraits are made without fail of all great rulers when they die. And there's a figure of the late Louis XIV. It was done by that greatly respected master Andre Benois, my teacher and instructor in this business, and that now in every European country, big and small, there is only one master left, and that is – me."

Saying that he prodded his chest with his finger and bowed with a broad and extravagant gesture to the 'duc' of Izhorsk, Danilych.

Danilych sat there calmly and asked the artist: "Is the figure lifesize?"

Rastrelli answered: "The figure is small, like the late king himself was small. It has a woman's mouth, and a nose like the beak of an eagle, but the lower lip is strong, and the chin distinguished. It is wearing lace and there is a mechanism to make it stand up and gesture with its arm in graceful welcome to visitors, because the figure is in a museum."

At this Danilych moved his hands as well: he knew little about construction, but he was fond of luxury, and he liked things. He did not like art, but he liked leisure. But as a matter of habit he asked, as though out of curiosity: "Is the machinery inside or is it fixed to the outside? Is it made of steel or iron, or what?"

But then he gave a dismissive wave of the hand, and said: "That's a stupid idea, to make the figure of such a person jump up and bid welcome to any old good-for-nothing. And anyhow I have no time now to listen to such a thing."

But after the brief translation of this Rastrelli grasped a fistful of air and proferred it to the prince: " It is good luck", he said, "for whoever manages to step forward before the wax figure stands up – all this is for good luck."

And then there was complete silence. Then the Prince of Izhorsk took out from a deep pocket a silver box, took out of it a silver toothpick, and began to pick his teeth.

"Is the wax from a forge, or left over from a cannon foundry? Is that any good for making such a figure?," he then asked.

Rastrelli answered proudly that no – it was no good. Really white wax was needed, but at that moment Mikhailovna entered "You have been summoned," she said, and Danilych, the most serene Prince, stood up ready to give his commands.

4

Two opposing winds were blowing along the Neva – a northerly, from the Swedes, and a damp one from the damp regions. The northerly was direct and curly-headed, but the damp wind was squint-eyed and bent. When they met there arose a third wind – a Finnish crosswind –a wind across everything. It blew in a whirlwind along the Neva, clearing small patches of snow, pushing snow up in the air like a grey beard, and then it blew against these patches, and covered them up again.

Then two young wolves dropped back from a big pack in the woods beyond Petrovsky Island. The two wolves ran along a tributary of the Neva. They jumped over it, and then stood and looked. Then they loped along Vassilevsky Island, along the new, straight road, the Line, and then once again they stopped. They had caught sight of a fisherman's straw hut and some wooden palings. In the hut was a human being, asleep, wrapped up. Then they made their way round the palings. They ran at even pace along the narrow path running-along the road. They skirted two mud huts, and opposite Menshikov's house they went down onto the Neva.

They stepped down carefully. There were piles of snow-covered rocks scattered about, and in places showing bare; they trod carefully, the wolves, and then ran in the direction of a sparse strip of woodland which they could see in the distance.

There was a light showing in one of the huts. It had indeed been showing earlier, only now it was clearer. Then, in the darkness, a man leapt out with some snarling dogs. He loosed the dogs, shouting as he did so, and soon he fired a shot from a long gun. Hans Jurgen had been a cook, and was now the river watchman, and he it was who had jumped out of his hut and fired the shot. The snarling dogs were his great dane hounds. He had twenty dogs altogether. Next the wolves pressed their hindquarters to the ice so that all their strength was transferred into their front paws. Their front paws got tighter and stronger, and the wolves began to gain distance, and they got away from the dogs.

Then they ran out onto the river bank, past the Letniy Sad and went as far as the Yerik, the little river of the Fontannaya. There they crossed the wide Nevsky Prospect road that goes to Novgorod. It was paved. There were boards stretched across it. Then, springing from tussock to tussock on the boggy ground, they disappeared into the thicket running along the Fontannaya stream.

The sound of a shot woke him.

5

All night he had been troubled in his sleep, dreaming disturbing dreams. And what disturbed him? The fate of the country. His arms dreamt they were carrying a burden, and he was restlessly carrying this burden from one place, and his legs were getting tired, growing thinner and thinner, and towards the end became like sticks.

He dreamt that the woman they call Yekaterina Alekseyevna, and he called darling Katerina, and was earlier called the dragoon's wife, Katerina Vasilyevskaya, and Skavronskaya, and Marta, and yet other names - he dreamt that she had left. He went into the palace and he wanted to run – everything seemed so empty without her, and there was a little bear wandering round the chambers. It was a docile animal, on a chain, with blackish fur, and great paws. And the bear was gentle with him. But Katerina had gone nobody knew where. Then there was a soldier, and a soldier's face, blown up, like a balloon. It was covered in tiny wrinkles, like ripples on water. And then he put down his burden and speared the soldier with his sword.

At this moment the bottom of his belly hurt, dragging it right down almost to the ground, but then this abated, though not altogether.

All the same he seized the soldier under the armpits, and began with his weak arms to search him. He spread him on the floor and brushed along his back with a hot broom. But the soldier lay quietly, and all around were household objects, and lots of them. As soon as he began to brush the soldier's back, his own back burned and he grew weak and changed. It grew cold and frightening, and he began to walk with his feet off the ground. And all the time the soldier was shouting in a high-pitched voice. And it was *his* voice – Peter's.

Then, far off, there was the boom of Swedish guns, and he woke up and realised that it was not he who was tormenting others, but he was being tormented. And he said, as though writing all this in a letter to Katerina: "Come and see how I am living, ill on my estate."

He woke up again and found himself in the dark, as though in a cocoon. It was stuffy. The room had been heated since the evening.

And he lay without a thought in his head.

He had even changed in stature. His legs were weak. His stomach was empty and hard as stone.

He decided not to record the dream he had had in the night in his study journal as he did normally. The dreams were not curious enough, and he was a little afraid of them. He was afraid of that soldier with wrinkles, and he did not know what the soldier signified. But he would have to find out about him.

Then it grew a little lighter in the room, as though a cook were stirring the mixture of the atmosphere with a spoon.

The day was beginning, and although he no longer did his tour of his affairs as soon as he awoke business matters occupied his thoughts, it seemed. In his mind he went into the workshop to turn something out of ivory. On the lathe there was an unturned block still remaining.

Then in his mind he went on an inspection tour to various places – today was Tuesday, not a ceremonial day. Some carriages were expected, and he would dress for all kinds of visits. He would put on his head his Kalmuk sheepskin hat and go to the Senate.

He would issue the following ukaz: not to make his temples tight more than once, and not to burn with a birch broom because if you do any more burning with birch twigs, then a person turns into you and you can lose yourself.

But these delirious thoughts of things to do quickly stopped without coming to an end, and having no beginning, like a shadow.

He became wide awake. The stove in his chamber had been heated since the evening before to such an extent that the glazed tiling was cracking and seemed to be about to burst in front of his eyes. The room was small and arid, and the very air was bursting from the heat, like the tiles.

Oh! If only the cool water of a fountain were to wet his little, dry head! If only the fountain were to concentrate and sweep over him with its jet, then his sickness would be washed away.

And when his whole body had woken up it realised that Pyotr Mikhailov was reaching his end, the final end and a quick one. At the very most he had a week to go. He would not agree to less. He was even afraid to think of less, and called himself Pyotr Mikhailov when he loved himself, or was sorry for himself.

And then his gaze became fixed on the light blue Dutch tiles which he had had sent from Holland. He had tried to introduce them in Russia, but without success. He looked at the stove which would be standing there long after him – a good solid stove.

Why hadn't these tiles been introduced here? He could not remember and looked at the tiles with a childlike gaze, free of any hidden thoughts.

A windmill.

A pavilion with a bridge.

And a three-masted ship.

And the sea.

A man in a round hat, pumping from a round pump, and three flowers, thick as human limbs.

A gardener.

A man passing with a jacket down to his waist is embracing a woman who seems to be enjoying it. A bit of fun on the journey!

A horse with a head like a dog.

A tree with curly branches like a Chinese tree.

A carriage with a person in it, and on the other side a tower, and a flag, and some birds flying.

A hut and along a path the figure of a young girl, big enough to make it unlikely that she could get into the hut, because she was depicted out of proportion.

A Dutch monk with a tonsure is sitting under a thorny tree, reading a book. He is wearing a thick sackcloth habit, and has his back turned.

And the sea.

A dovecote, simple with little columns thick like knees. And there are statues and vases. There is a dog in the background with a woman's face, barking. A bird from the side looks like it is swimming with its wings.

A cool Chinese pagoda.

Two fat people on a bridge. The bridge is on piles like the spines of book bindings. A Dutch custom.

There is another bridge, a lifting one on chains. The channel underneath is rounded.

There is a tower and from its top is let down a hook. On the hook is a rope, and on the hook is dangling a load. It is being hauled up.

Below, in a canal is a boat and three oarsmen. They wear round hats and they are transporting a cow in the boat. And the cow is drawn with a big head and has speckled markings.

A shepherd is herding a flock of horned animals, and on a hill there are some spiky trees with furry leaves, like a dog's coat. It is hot summer.

A castle, one of the square old-fashioned kind. On an inlet there are some ducks swimmimg, and a tree is leaning over. North-east.

And the sea.

A half destroyed building or a ruin. And a troop of horsemen is riding along the sand, and some tree trunks are bare, and the tents have horns.

And there is a three-masted ship on the sea.

And farewell ship, farewell stove!

And farewell splendid palaces! No longer shall I walk through you.

Farewell barge, my dear old barge!

I shall not be sailing to the Senate on you!

Don't wait for me! Pay off the crew!

Farewell my jacket with the sword-belt!

My kaftan!

My slippers!

Farewell sea! Angry one!

Sails as well, farewell!

Farewell, ropes smeared with pitch!

Sea wind. Oysters!

The sail-making. The dockyards, farewell!

Navigation and the armoury!

And farewell, you.

And you also, farewell, wool beating and fulling!

And making uniforms!

Also farewell prospecting and the mines, deep and airless!

I should go to the lathering room and have a good steam!

The doctors had forbidden him drinking malvasin.

Also farewell the Admirals Hour and the 'osteriya'[05], and the free house and the bawdy houses and the willing women, and their white legs, and the homely fun – such enjoyable work!

---

[05]   *Tavern*

Peterhof garden, farewell! The superb hornbeams, and the limes from Amsterdam!

Farewell, my lords from foreign lands – the Swedish lion and the Chinese dragon. And farewell also you sizeable ship!

I don't know who will have you!

My sons and little daughters, the little squids, have all died out, and the biggest scoundrel I put away myself!

They all led to nothing!

Farewell, Piter Baas[06], honourable captain of the bombardier company. Pyotr Mikhailov!

I am dying from some wicked, secret internal illness!

And I don't know to whom I shall leave the country, the economy and art!

He wept silently into the bedspread, and the bedspread was made of scraps, many scraps, velvet, silk and fustian, and like those of country children, it was warm. It was damp along the bottom edge.

His bonnet had slipped off his broad head. His hair was close cropped, like a soldier's, shaven at the forehead.

His camisole was hanging on its hanger, put up long ago. The time for use had passed, and it had grown decrepit. It was no longer fit for service.

In an hour's time Katerina would come, and he was dying because he had not executed her, and was even letting her into his chamber.

He ought to have had her executed, then his blood would have felt better, and he would have recovered. And now his blood was going

---

[06]   Master Peter (Dutch). It was Peter's guild title

to his lower parts, and it was held up, holding and would not let go.

He had not had his crony, Danilych, executed, and he felt no better for that. And the man in the little chamber next door had fallen silent. The scratching of his pen and his muttering over the accounts had gone. And he would not manage to get the axe to fall on that scrawny neck either.

He had obviously been sent away, that man in the neighbouring room. There was no longer anyone to listen to his reports.

His time had passed. They had sold him off, the soldier's son, Pyotr Mikhailov!

His lips began to tremble, and his head to toss on his pillow. It lay there, swarthy skinned, not all that big, wIth knitted brows, just as seven years earlier had lain the head of that other broad-shouldered soldier's son, the head of Aleksei, the son of Petrov.

And there was no real anger. Anger did not come, only shuddering. If he had been able to get angry he would have got angry and the mistress would have come and tickled the top of his head. Then he would have woken up, then got better.

At that moment onto the tower from which a load was hanging on a rope, onto the blue tile – there crawled out a stove cockroach. It crawled out, then stopped and looked.

In his life he had had three fears, and they were all big ones: the first was fear of water, the second fear of blood.

He had been afraid of water as a child. His gorge rose at the sight of this murky liquid, and from the movement of deep waters.

Nevertheless, he was fond of his small boat, because it had sides to protect him from high water. He had got used to it, and enjoyed it.

He was afraid of blood, but not for long. As a child he had watched his uncle being killed, and his uncle was so red, and his skin stripped away all over. It was like a carcass in the meat market, yet his uncle's face was white as though a decorator had painted it. There was blood instead of eyes, and at that time he had felt fear and trembling, but there was a certain degree of curiosity. And the curiosity dominated, and he was curious about blood.

And the third fear was that filthy wretch, the krinkly cockroach.And that fear had not left him.

But, after all, what was all the fuss about, that he should be so frightened of it? Nothing.

It had first appeared just under fifty years ago. It had come from Turkey in a great swarm infiltrating the abortive Turkish campaign. It bred in the hostelries, both where it was damp and where it was dry. Or perhaps it had been breeding in cracks and crevices, secretly hiding, being there all the time, and then suddenly creeping out? Or was it its Chinese whiskers? It had looked like Fyodor Yurich, the Kaiser-Pope, like Prince Romadonovsky, with its Chinese whiskers. Or was it that it was hollow and when squashed made a crunching noise, like an empty container or a fish bubble? Or even because when it was dead it was all flat, like the sole of the foot. Or maybe he did not like it because it was some filth from the land of the Turks?

Whenever they had to travel anywhere scouts and couriers went on ahead, looking at the houses to find where they could stop and whether or not it was infested with vermin. Without doing that they would not stop anywhere – against infection there was no deterrent or defence.

And now he, Peter, was crying. His eyes were full of tears and he could not see the insect. But when he had wiped his eyes with the bedcover then he could see it.

The cockroach stood there, waggling its antennae and looking. It had a black sheen on it, like an olive. Where were those forty times forty legs going? Where were they going to rustle off to? What if it jumps onto the bed and goes on to crawl all over the bedcover? Then his toes grew weak, he began to shiver, and he pulled the bedcover up round his nose. Then he freed his arm from beneath it to stretch out for a shoe to throw at the insect. But there were no shoes there, only slippers, which were too soft and would not kill it while it was standing there and not hiding. Nevertheless he stretched for it, but could not reach and began to crawl on his hands and elbows. How weak they were! They would not take his weight! And his chest felt like a mattress filled with rubbish. Then he lay there, resting. Then he crawled as far as some armchairs on his hands and elbows. The chairs were oak ones, turned, with their arms fashioned like those of a woman. For a last time he grasped at the fine oak fingers, and then his arm, as though he were swimming, hung in the air, still reaching for the slippers. But the slippers were not there, and there was no floor, and his arm was floating. Then his teeth began to chatter, because he could no longer watch the cockroach, and it was waiting for him, and maybe had dropped down and was already on the move. And all of a sudden the cockroach really did fall, as though dead. It hit the floor and lay there. And they were both in the same state. Pyotr Alekseyevich was unconscious – out to the world, as though dead drunk. His strength had given out. But he was patient, and still tried to come round, and eventually did.

He turned round, eyes staring, looking all around – Where had the wicked insect gone? His eyes were weak. He directed his gaze at a point above the varnished dado, and then caught sight of a strange face. The person was sitting to the left of the bed, by the doorway, on a little bench. He was young, and his eyes were staring at him, Peter, and his teeth were chattering and his head shaking, either he was uncivilised, or cold, or an idiot. Next to him sat an old man. He was asleep. His face looked rather like that of Musin-Pushkin, from the senate. From the younger one's face he looked to be German, from Holstein.

Then Peter looked again and saw the young man's teeth chattering, and his lips apparently trembling, but that he was not an idiot, and he said weakly: "Ei! Dat is nit permittert!"

He was ashamed that the Holsteiner was seeing him like this, and that the man had got into his bedchamber.

But at the same time his fear had diminished.

And when he glanced at the stove the cockroach was not there anymore, and he had been deceiving himself, and had imagined it.

How could there be a cockroach here? For a while he grew weak and drifted off, and when he opened his eyes he could see three people. None of them was asleep, and the young one whom he had imagined to be a Holsteiner was also a senator, Dolgoruky.

He said: "Who's there?"

Then the old man and the other two stood up and the old man said, placing his arms at his side: "We have been detailed to keep watch on your Majesty's health."

He shut his eyes and dozed.

He did not know that from this night on three senators had been given the task of keeping watch in the bedchamber. Then, without looking at them, he gave a dismissive wave of the hand: "Later."

And all three left the room.

And that same night, in that little chamber which was next to the bedchamber there sat at a table a short man, pockmarked, broad in the face and insignificant looking. He was rustling through some papers. All the papers were laid out in order, so that at any time he could take them into the bedchamber and give his report on them.

That night the man was busy with these papers. He was the Officer General Fiscal, and was drawing up his report. His first name was Aleksei and his family name was Myakinin, not one of the old established families. He had gathered in the papers from the fiscal officers, and the calmest of these was the merchant fiscal officer, Busarevsky. He would write on the state of a project, if it was suitable or not, what had been given (as bribes) and what taken, and what had been squirreled away in unexpected places. He had a fine nose for gifts, for bribery a superior nose, and for non-declaration an inferior one. And with the onset of the illness this insignificant man had been summoned, and told – be near at hand, in the little chamber next my bed-chamber, because I can no longer get to where you are. And you sit and write and report to me. They will serve you your supper in this little room. Just sit and keep out of sight. Just keep out of sight and write.

And after that, every day, the little room resounded to the click and clack as the man recorded wholesale figures on an abacus. And on the morning of the second day the man came secretively into the bedchamber and made his report. After this report Pyotr's lips began to quiver and his mouth foamed. The little man stood and waited. He was patient and waited with his head on one side. He was a nondescript little man. Then, when the lip-trembling had ceased, the man lifted his head. The forehead was creased with wrinkles, and he directed his gaze to the Imperial Personage himself, looking into his very eyes. His look was simple, his eyelashes were ginger, this look was worldly-wise. Then the man asked in a low voice, like the voice used to address a sick person or someone whose house and possessions have been burnt in a fire:

"What do you say – should I flog just with birches?"

But the mouth remained motionless, no longer trembling, and answered not a word. The eyes were closed, and probably some sort of secret inner struggle had commenced. At this point the pock-faced man thought that he had not made himself heard, and he asked even more quietly:

"Do you want me to apply the axe to the whole tree?"

But the man in the bed remained silent so he still stood there with all his papers. The pock-faced one, the nothing man, Myakinin, Aleksey.

Then the eyes opened, and a thin voice, with a crack in it said to Aleksey Myakinin

"Cut it right out."

And one eye looked fearfully at Myakinin. It seemed as though Myakinin might be showing pity. But the latter stood there – ginger-haired, a flush of colour in his face, a small man, peaceable, it was his job.

And now the man was collating everything and sewing it all together with a thick needle, and in the morning he would report – face to face. The bundle of papers was already thick. Busarevsky came to him, the merchant finance officer – there was a decree to admit this man at any time whatever.

And when the merchant officer fiscal had gone Myakinin at once broke into a sweat, and he sweated for a long time. He wiped his forehead with his hand, but his hands were sweating as well. Then he sat down, checked a couple of times more on the abacus and then scratched with his pen again. The first papers referred to the gracious Prince Izhorsky. When he had done scratching he sewed some top papers to it. The top papers had been drawn up before-hand, about the sizeable sums his Excellency had transferred to

Amsterdam and Lyons banks, but these top papers remained top papers. But to it he sewed yet another, a very top paper, also about the significant sums his Excellency had deposited in Amsterdam and Lyons. Very considerable sums. And he was sweating because these sizeable sums had been sent to Dutch Amsterdam and French Lyons through his Excellency by none other than Her Imperial Majesty. He was sweating all over. And then at one and the same time sewed on some information about the hitherto unknown and secret gifts given through Vilim Ivanovich to Her Majesty. He didn't draw up a separate file but simply he sewed it to the first one. He was sweating and did not know how to act, whether to draw up a special file or not. And after he had stitched them together he looked through the papers with an anxious eye. He calculated on the abacus and the beads at once showed many thousands. Countless thousands! He slid everything over, so that the beads showed nothing.

Then, leafing through the multiple sheets of paper with one plump finger, which he kept licking, he made the addition, calculated, and it all came out to: 92. He looked at it for a long while, and then his brow furrowed and his eyes stared in amazement. Then with a quick sudden movement he pushed one bead up – made a subtraction – and was left with: 91. And he grasped, this time even with three fingers, at this last bead and it burnt his finger so, that in the end he clumsily pulled it back.

Then he put his hand to his close cropped hair, took a handful of hair and began to run his fingers through it. Then at once he placed the accounts on the floor.

Then he went to bed.

Yet there were 92 beads – 92 beads.

And in the morning he went to report. He in the other room was asleep. The man remained standing there. Then one eye was open, which gave the signal that he was listening.

And in a quiet voice, not even a proper voice, but some kind of inner rumbling right next to the ear of the man in the bed, he made his report. But the eye was closed again, and Myakinin saw that Peter was lying there unconscious, and he stood hesitantly waiting. But then a tear rolled down and this tear gave the sign that Myakinin had been heard. But the fingers made another signal, and this one Myakinin did not understand: it was not quite – go away, not quite – do nothing until further investigation, or it could have been – forget it, or – it doesn't matter any more.

And so he did not understand, but he went off to his little chamber. His pen no longer scratched and he pushed the accounts aside with his foot. And that day someone forgot to bring him any food. So he sat there hungry and did not go to bed. Then he heard a sound: something was not right, someone was trying to get in and was making a rustling noise, like in a hayloft, then everything went quiet – all the same something was up. Towards morning he very quickly pulled apart everything he had sewn together, tore it to pieces and, looking round, thrust them into his shoe, but he jotted down the figures of his calculations in an unaccustomed place, so that if need be he could recreate them, and make his report.

An hour later the door was pushed open and in came Katerina, Her Majesty. At this Myakinin Aleksey stood to attention. Her Majesty indicated with her finger that he should leave. He was about to reach for his papers, but at this she put her hand on them and started to read them. And Myakinin Aleksei, without a word, left the room. When he got home he burnt in the stove all that he had thrust into his shoe. But the calculations remained in an unmarked place, where no-one could grasp them.

And quite a few files were left in the little chamber. There was a paper about appropriations from ships and boats that had been built – it was about Admiral General Apraksin. And there were papers about almost all the gentlemen from the Senate, who had taken what and for what. But this was only with reference to the large-scale bribes and appropriations, there was little room to write about the lesser offences. About how the merchants were concealing their profits. About the brothers Shustov, who still owed many thousands in tax while they themselves had gone missing, and were wandering around who knows where, disguised as beggars. How members of the nobility were concealing their grain, and waiting to get more money when food ran short – their names were all there, and much more besides. There were the papers and Myakinin just could not think what to do with them.

He was red-haired, broad browed, not a superior looking gentleman. If it had not been for Pavel Ivanovich Yaguzhinsky he would probably not have sat for ages in that little room, and he would not have been chased out of it by the Empress Katerina herself.

Towards morning three senators went into the Senate, they convened it and issued an ukaz[07]:

To release many convicts who had been transported to hard labour, that they should be free to pray for the lasting health of His Majesty. It was the start of much business: the Master was still speaking but could no longer get fiercely angry. That night Danilych, Prince of Izhorsk, was summoned. And the latter, already at the Grand Palace, sent for his military secretary, Vust, and told him to double the watch in the city at once. Vust at once doubled it.

And then everyone knew that He would soon be dead.

7

But they knew about this even earlier in the particular place where they know everything – in the tavern, the Fortuna, situated in an out of the way spot.

The 'Fortuna' stood in front of the Admiralty. It had been set up for the foreign workmen who were homesick. The workmen missed their own country where they had been born. Or they were missing their wife and the children they would chastise when they were at home, or they missed their household possessions, or perhaps one particular object they had left behind. They really missed all this in

[07]   *Imperial edict*

30

this unfamiliar and hazardous place.

There in the tavern there was beer by the mugful or by the cask, and many people came there, both singly and in groups. They would drink from the tubs out of ladles. Then they would wipe their mouth and give a great sigh: "Aaach!"

Everyone went to this crowded place – the tavern.

Above the Fortuna on the roof was a pole on which was the national bird, the eagle. It was made of metal with a pattern on it. It was bent by the wind, and rusty, and they had begun to call it the Cockerel.

Because of the bird the Fortuna was visible from a huge distance away, even from the great swamp with the birch grove around the Nevsky Prospect Road. Everyone would say, let's go to the old cock. Because the cockerel – that's a bird, but the old cock meant getting soused. Lots of people knew each other here, just like meeting on the street, because in Petersburk[08] everyone had a standing. But there were also those with no name: Petersburk bargemen. They were proper drunkards.

The hardened drinkers would be standing near the entrance at the barrels. They would drink barefoot, taking their boots off and hanging them tidily on the cask. Because of that the air smelt of balsam. They drank beer, homebrew, and what flowed down their whiskers back into the cask others would scoop out of the cask and drink after them.

It was quiet there with just the sound of slurping, and the occasional grunt of enjoyment.

Ach!

In the first room there were all kinds of loudmouthed drunkards. They roared with laughter as they drank – they cared for nothing. They were having a good time. From the corners of the room there

[08]   Contemporary spelling based on contemporary pronunciation

came shouts of

- Spades!

- Clubs!

Because here they were playing cards, or dice, and other obscenities, occasionally fights broke out.

And further on, in a smaller room with one window were people of the middling sort, more refined intellectuals, middle rank government officials, skilled artisans, Swedes, Frenchmen and Dutchmen. And also soldiers' wives, dragoons' widows, women ready for some fun.

Here they were drinking in silence, not fooling around. Only the odd one was singing. Here were the people who were most fed up. In the entrance area the language was Russian and Swedish. In the second room there was a jumble of tongues. From the farthest room the languages spread into the first, and then into the entrance area, and from the tavern the sounds of the languages reached the brick and daub cottages and the very swamp itself.

And although the language differed, Swedish, German, Turkish, French and Russian, everyone was drinking in Russian and cursing in Russian. That's what the business of the tavern was all about.

The conversation in French was: the memory of wine, and the man who could remember the most kinds of wine gained the most respect, because he was an experienced wine drinker, and knew life in his home country.

Legendre, the assistant, said:

"Just now I would take a bottle of Pantaque, then a half bottle of Bastrou, then a small glass of Frontenac, and perhaps a small glass of Muscatel as well. That's what I always served in Paris."

But Leblanc, the carpenter, having heard this, said to him:

"No, I don't like Frontenac. I only drink St Laurent, Alcan, Portuguese, and sparkling Canary. But most of all I enjoy Hermitage. I used to serve it to guests in Paris, and everyone liked it."

Struck by such a rude reply from Leblanc, the carpenter, the assistant Legendre downed a glass of vodka. He then asked Leblanc, giving him an enquiring look:

"Do you like arak?"

"No, I don't like arak, and I don't drink spirits at all," rejoined Leblanc.

"Oh!" then said Legendre, the assistant, already in a sharp tone, "Yesterday, monsieur Pinot, the craftsman, entertained me with arak, chocolate, and we smoked Virginian tobacco together!"

And he drained a mug of beer.

But now Leblanc started to get worked up. He stared Legendre full in the face, furious, and his whiskers stuck out either side, like a walrus.

"Pinot", he exclaimed. "Pinot is the same kind of craftsman as me, and I am the same as Pinot. Only he carves only shells and grotesques, whereas I carve everything, and I also turn things for your boss. Things for which I don't even know the name or purpose, damn me!"

And these last words Leblanc, the carpenter, said in Russian.

Legendre was happy with such words from the carpenter, and with the fact that the artistic woodworker had got angry.

"And did you, monsieur Leblanc, get that piece of oak from the count, d'you remember? That off-cut of best oak for carving. We discussed it with the count, didn't we?"

"I didn't," said Leblanc, "because I'm not a coffin maker, but a carver of architecture, and in these parts they only use oak for coffins, and besides, it's against the law, and no one will sell it, damn it!" – and these last words were said in Russian.

He was not drinking beer, but vodka all the time, and now he began to get violent and, grasping Legendre by the lapels, began shaking him.

"If you don't tell me why your count is buying up a lot of wax, while I am looking all over for oak – I shall go to the authorities, and I shall tell them, damn it, that you are helping in the making of casting moulds for illegal coinage, and then perhaps you'll enjoy the supplice des batognes[09] or the grand knout!"

Then the assistant Legendre became calmer, and said quietly:

"The wax is for the arms and legs, and the oak is for the torso."

Then they fell silent and Leblanc began to ponder and look at Legendre. He thought for some time, and when he had done so he said calmly:

"Oh, so the powers that be are already getting ready to send him to his forefathers? Don't worry, I've made a torso like that before".

Then he wiped his whiskers and said:

"None of this really concerns me. I'm a straightforward kind of person, and I don't like people who are devious. I'll give you a bottle of Florentine, and a packet of Brazilian tobacco. It's better than Virginian. This has nothing to do with me. I'm going to earn three thousand francs more and then I'm going to leave this country. Pinot is the same kind of craftsman as me, except that he carves shells, while I carve everything. And I carve in stone, which you might have known if you were interested, and he only carves in wood. And oak like that is really difficult to find.

---

[09] *Running the gauntlet*

At this point Legendre, the assistant, began to whistle and sing in a thin voice a French song about la-la –la going into the woods and meeting a young girl, and he starts to pinch her more and more, and all over until she is quite la-la-la. Leblanc meanwhile began talking about a wood called sassafras which is not to be found in Russia.

Then he wept and began to declaim from Philipe Deport's ode of farewell to Poland:

"Adieu! Pays d'un eternal adieu!"

Because in his mind's eye he could see himself earning his thousands of francs (and not three thousand, but fifteen in all), and how he would go to the city of Paris, and leave this swamp. And as for Poland and Russia, he could not care less.

And then in the second room there appeared Ivanko the Tooth, also known as Ivanko Zhuzla, or the Pipe, or Ivan Zhmakin. He went through to the second room with a light and easy tread. He looked in to see who was there, and what was going on and was on his way past when he was stopped by a master tailor, who said:

"Stop a minute. I know your face. Aren't you one of the master tailors?"

"You've guessed it", said Ivanko, "Indeed I am a master tailor. What's that German singing about then?"

And he nodded in the direction of Legendre, and winked to a coachman that he knew who was dipping into some kvass, and then he drifted out again with his light and easy tread.

And at the second table there really was a German sitting and singing a German song. It was the apothecary's assistant, Balthasar Stahl. He had come from the Kikin Palace, from the Kunstkammer[10]. He was so thin and tall, and his face so covered in freckles that he was known

---

[10]   Chamber of curiosities (German) building housing Peter's collection of art objects and objects of curiosity

all over Petersburk. He did not visit the tavern often. He had a job at the Kunstkammer, renewing the spirit in the specimen jars. These specimens consumed up to a hundred pails of spirit a year as a result of which they sat in fumes. And, because he changed the spirit, he, the assistant apothecary, was permeated with this smell. Now he was sitting in the tavern, and opposite him sat another assistant.

He was with the well-known apothecary, Liphold from the doctors' pharmacy, from Tsaritsyn Field, and he was a long-time German[11], almost Russian so to speak. His father had been born in the Moscow German quarter, and so he was styled an old German, but he was still a young man.

Herr Balthasar had been singing a song about how sometimes he stood, then he would walk he didn't know where, and finally he explained to his friend, another old German, that the reason why he had come to the tavern was because the human exhibits had drunk all the spirit. He had sworn at them. There were in all four human freak exhibits, and the main and most intelligent one was Yakov. Which is why Balthasar had put him in charge of all the other freaks who were more cretinous. It never happened with him that he brutalised or abused them, even up to the great drinking bout of the evening before, when he, Balthasar Stahl, found towards morning all the freaks almost ill from disgusting drunkenness, and nevertheless had to take care of them, because they were precious exhibits.

Then the old German said: "Tch! Tch!" by which it could be understood that he appreciated the difficult position Balthasar was in, and blamed the freaks.

And today, Balthasar said, because Herr Schuhmacher was abroad, and he, Balthasar was deputising for this great man of science (and this was a matter of great importance to the state, but better not to talk of it for in two of the jars they had there were two human heads which must not be mentioned, and if these exhibits got spoilt, then something that does not bear thinking about would happen) – and he had been to the apartments of the apothecary Blumentrost to

[11]   The adjective was used for many foreign craftsmen working for Peter

give his report and ask for more spirit, as the freaks had drained his earlier supply to the last drop.

At this juncture the old German said:"Oh!" and at the same time expressed the thought that he had a great respect for well-known persons, and was sorry that they had to put themselves out for the sake of some freaks, but that he did not need to know the details about any state heads.

"And what did the Kunstkammer secretary do?", Balthasar suddenly asked him.

"He shoved my reports under the ink well, and shouted at me and stamped his foot. He said it was not the time to talk about the freaks when the Tsar was gravely ill – and then 'raus! raus!' and he pushed me out of the door, and that's how the tragic scene was played out."

"Tsss!", said the old German, and shook his head, indicating that although he thought Balthasar was right, yet who he was to criticise people of high standing.

Then he said, guiding the conversation away from such sensitive topics:

"Yes, of course, of course; although it does seem as though the person at the top there is seriously ill, and Herr Liphold told me that the doctors have already sent to Holland for a consilium medicum from Herr Boorgav, because the doctors here cannot find a cure".

Then Herr Balthazar Stahl, now quite calm, raised one finger, and said quietly, "It will be interesting to see what kind of interregnum there will be here. But better not to discuss it. Herr Menschenkopf[12], that's who will be in charge, I'll wager, but not a word more about it."

But when he glanced at the old German there was no one sitting opposite him. But the old German was like that. Scared by the inappropriate conversation, he had already slipped back into the first

---

[12]   Mr. Human Head (German) contortion of Menshikov's family name

room.

But in the first room there was a fisherman sitting and drinking. At that moment Ivanko walked past, and the fisherman stopped him, stared at him, and said:

"Stop. I seem to know you. You look familiar. Didn't you use to fish on the Volga?"

"You've guessed right," said Ivanko, and his eyes narrowed, "I've fished on the Volga. That was me."

Then, with his easy gait, he pushed his way into one corner of the room, and sat down at a table, beneath which was a pool of melting snow from everyone's boots. A varied selection of people were sitting at the table.

"I can have a laugh here", said Ivanko quietly to himself, "these people are not too clever."

Almost all the people at the table, when they caught sight of Ivanko, drifted away so that only three remained. To these three Ivanko said: "now there'll be some fun. The cat's not going to die in autumn, or on a Tuesday, or Wednesday, but on a grey Friday. In the Yamskaya area horses have already been got together. They were trotted over from the posting yard. They'll be used to bring news of his death to Germanland[13] I see it as a joke, all sorts of queer people are suddenly coming out of the woodwork. And tomorrow they'll all be let out."

And the three asked, "Who?"

"They'll release," responded Ivanko, "the master tailors, those that sew with an oaken needle. And they'll also release to all the four winds the Volga fishermen – those that catch fish with hooks and nets. They'll let them all out tomorrow – there's the market. There's the gaol, and stand to attention! I think it's comic, you queer people!"

[13] *any territory west of Poland*

Then one of the three, with long hair, probably a defrocked priest, suddenly at the table still let out a hoarse cry of:

"He's dying from smoking that tobacco pipe!"

Very soon there came into the tavern Mr Police Captain, followed by two guards armed with pikes and rattles. And the captain read out an ukaz: the tavern was to be closed to mark many years of good health for the Tsar. He then drank from the barrel, and the watchmen did so too. And everyone left, all those who had already seen this coming, all the craftsmen who were homesick, and the Germans, and the Dutch skippers, and the coachmen – all manner of people.

Chapter Two

"Is it not better to live than to die?"

VYMENEY, KING OF THE SAMOYEDS

It was not a large section in the Kunstkammer. It occupied just one small room to begin with. The collection had originated in Moscow. Then it had moved to the Summer Palace, in Petersburk. Here there were two small rooms. Then it became the Kunstkammer, a stone built house. It was separate from the other sections in the Smolny. Here everything had been brought together, the live exhibits and the dead ones, and the guard had his own little cottage attached to the main building. There were three guards. One was responsible for the exhibits in jars, another for the stuffed animals, keeping them clean, and the third for cleaning the rooms generally. Then, when Aleksei Petrovich was executed for some important crime, the whole Kunstkammer, lock stock and barrel, both natural and unnatural exhibits, was moved to the Liteiny – to the Kikin Palace. So the exhibits had been moved from place to place. But now they were quite remote, and it was not so easy, not so convenient, for people to drive or walk there. People were not so willing to come. So then they started to put up little 'Kunsthouses' on the main square, so that they could be seen from all angles, with the buildings of all the collegia, on the other side with the fortress, and now on the third side the 'Kunsthouses'. But for the moment not many people visited the Kikin house. It was not so convenient. Then they thought up the idea of making sure that every visitor to the palace was given something as hospitality. Visitors were served either a cup of coffee, or a glass of vodka, or Hungarian wine. To go with it they were offered zuckerbrot. Yagushinsky, the Procurator General, proposed that everyone wanting to view the collection should pay a rouble entrance fee. The money collected would pay for the keep of the freaks. But this was not taken up and zuckerbrot and vodka were dispensed for free. Then a noticeably larger number of people started to visit the Kunstkammer, and two scriveners, one junior and the other somewhat more senior, even began to turn up twice a day. But then they were rarely offered vodka, and never given zuckerbrots. instead they were offered a bread roll or a pretzel, and sometimes a small white loaf, and sometimes they were not offered anything at all. These scriveners lived in one of the nearby cottages.

They were always accompanied round the Kunskammer (in case they damaged or stole anything) by the deputy librarian or one of the guards, or the head freak – Yakov. The latter was also the stoker and took care of the stove. It was always warm in the Kikin House.

2

Infants, their bodies golden with fat, lemon coloured, were swimming in the jars of spirit, with their little arms, and pushing themselves with their little legs, like frogs in water. And next to them were some heads, also in jars. And they had their eyes open. They were all about a year or two old. And these heads gazed with living eyes, blue, the colour of cornflowers, dark, human eyes . And where the head had been severed you would almost think that at any moment blood would spurt forth. That was how well everything had been preserved by the alchohol.

PUERIS CAPUT NO.70

The head was swarthy skinned. The eyes were squinting with displeasure, and the brows were slanting. The nose was short. The forehead was broad and the chin sharp. And this yellow coloured head was important, and the child was supposed to be a Mongol prince. It had a peaceful air about it and the unsmiling lips were drooping. This infant had been brought over from the Pyotr-Pavlovsk fortress. It was not known from which cell, or who the mother was. There were three women in the cells at that time. The third one was a young Finnish woman, known as Yefrosinya Fyodorova. She had been imprisoned as a result of the affair of Aleksey Petrovich, the tsarevich, Peter's son. And she had been his mistress, and had betrayed him. She had given birth in the fortress. The head looked round at everything with its heavy eyelids. It looked with displeasure, importantly, just like a little Mongol prince – as though squinting from the bright sun.

The House was a large one, and it caught the sun all day. The rain outside the windows was not frightening. It was warm and there were various objects scattered about:

Monsieur le bourgeois

He was a giant, French by birth from the town of Calais, a footman and a drunkard. He had been added to the collection because of his height. He was a sazhen and three vershki tall[14]. They had tried for a long time to find him a wife who was equally tall. They wanted to see what would come from such a union. Perhaps they might get a race of giants. But nothing came of it – he was a tall drunkard, and had no other value. He produced a son and two daughters. They were of normal height. But when he died from venereal disease they had skinned him. For Ryush the foreigner Yenmou had undertaken to do it. He boasted a lot about it and held on to the skin for about a year, would not give it back and just kept asking for money and making a fuss. The bourgeois himself was disembowelled, and the stomach preserved in spirit. It was the size of a bull's. It was in a jar in a cupboard, and in addition there stood monsieur le bourgeois' skeleton. It was huge and what was the most curious of all it was riddled with venereal disease, like wormholes. So that monsieur le bourgeois was there in three forms: his skin (courtesy of the craftsman Henshaw), his stomach (in a jar), and his free-standing skeleton.

And in the third chamber were the animals, and everyone on coming in and seeing them thought: what splendid plump animals in this to them foreign land!

The animals stood there, dark and glistening, with sharp beaks and blunt muzzles, and their muzzles were like the light at dusk and looked, and looked out through the glass walls around them. They had come from all the ends of the earth. Their coats were glistening rich, Westerners!

A monkey sat calmly in a jar. Its face was lilac coloured and severe. It

---

[14]   *Seven foot, five and a half inches*

looked like a catholic saint.

On some tables were arranged mineral samples, glistening with an earthy sparkle. And some fossilised bread from Copenhagen.

And everyone who entered looked at the cabinets and was lost in wonder: what a collection! Then they would make their way straight to the animals that were standing outside the cabinets. Free-standing, not in cabinets, were Russian animals, or at least those that had died here on Russian soil.

There was a Siberian white sable and some lizards.

The Elephant

He was standing in front of a white building, and all around him were people shouting in chorus, like monkeys:

"Shah inshalah!"

And then they fell on their knees.

Then he started to climb some steps. His ears were heavy with gold, and his sides were covered in little suns. All around was air and below his feet were broad and grey and warm. And when he had reached the top of the stairs his keeper shouted a word in elephant language and he bent down and knelt in front of some person:

"Shah inshalah! Hussein!"

Then there was reed straw strewn beneath his feet, water on his lips and his regular food.

Then there came for him a Persian, an arab, and some Armenians in rich clothes, and after that his life became full of noise and disturbance.

He did not know that the Persian had been sent a gift, and that he was that gift. He could not know that the Ottoman, Hussein, the Persian and Peter of Moscow were squabbling over the Caucasus, that Kabardin and the Kumytsk khans and the Kuban horde were involved. He could not know who supported whom, and why they were constantly changing sides. Then he was floating, standing on some planks, and the water smelt. And so he reached the city of Astrakhan. Once more there were crowds of people, and camels and shouting. And when he was led along the street – and he walked slowly – people threw themselves on their knees before him and wiped their foreheads in the dust. But he walked slowly, like a god.

Then they left the city of Astrakhan, and many people with bundles followed him, like pilgrims. Now already the cold time began – there was much water. There was no reed straw, no flies, an empty time, and many things disappeared. Now already he was entering an unknown country. Then they led him to a town which was not a town, where there were houses and no houses, no boats, sometimes sky, sometimes not. They led him to a wooden building, shouted an elephant word, and once more he knelt before someone.

Then the water began to hum, and it went on humming many times.

But he walked slowly, like a god, but no one fell to their knees before him. And there, where he slept, it smelt of unfamiliar, bitter wood. It was a grey time. He had vodka on his lips, rice in his mouth, and there were no reeds beneath his feet. He saw no more elephants, only non-elephants. Then the time became more frosty and crackling. The wind moaned in the tops of the trees, hoarse seeming – alien. He did not know, could not know, that it was called the Northerly. It made things not a little cold, and the elephant shivered.

Then the elephant began to stop missing other elephants, and began to miss non-elephants, because even they stopped coming to see him.

And when it grew warmer they led him out from the animal enclosure, and many non-elephants began to throw sticks and stones at him. Then the elephant grew frightened and began to run around like a young one. And all around people whistled and stamped their feet and laughed at him.

At night the elephant did not sleep. When evening came the guards gave him vodka. And then in the neighbouring room he could hear dull breathing and a long, drawn out roar. He listened. It was a lion breathing. And he could not know that this next door was also a present from the Shah. To be precise, a lion and a lioness; he was drunk and got up, broke his chain, and went out into the garden. There were no trees in it, just a fence. Then he broke down the fence and got out onto Vassilevsky Island. Once there he set off down the road like a mindless juvenile. People came running after him and he quickened his pace. They threw rocks, logs, stones and planks at him. When it began to hurt him a red mist came over his eyes, and he raised his trunk and advanced as though he was in formation with lots of other elephants alongside him. He smashed up the Finnish village, and that was where they caught him and kicked him in the flanks. Then they led him back again to the animal enclosure. Less and less non-elephants came, and he saw their eyes less and less frequently. And the last non-elephant was often unsteady on his feet, and shouted like an ape and kicked the elephant in the belly. And his trunk hung like the wind, and it was too much effort to stand up and drive away this last ape.

Then they started to feed him less. His body shrank from too little food, and his grey skin hung on him like a cotton dress on an old woman. His eyes were cloudy and red and not like eyes at all. He walked unsteadily and his innards shook. How vast they were! Then he grew flabby and became like the dirty drunk that guarded him, only that you could see his breathing from his flanks.

Then he died. They removed his skin and stuffed it. He became an exhibit.

Various minerals from all over the earth lay around on display tables.

Nearby stood an African donkey – a zebra. Its skin was striped like a Kalmuck robe.

Walrus.

Dzhigitey, the Lapland reindeer.

The great Samoyed leader had sent riders to St Petersburg, and they were mounted on reindeer and set up camp on Petrov Island. There there were plenty of trees and sufficient moss. Once they lighted a big fire and danced and clapped their hands and sang. Dzhigitey could not know that the Samoyed chief had died, and was no more. Dzhigitey could only smell the smoke. Then they came to Dzhigitey:

Dzhigitey-ey-ey!

He got the wind in his mouth, and Dzhigitey ate it instead of the moss, until he felt ill from eating too much. But they still pressed his flanks and the reins went on singing. He ate and ate the wind until he could no more.

And when he had galloped to a particular place all around him they shouted:

" Chief of the Samoyeds!"

And they took off his traces and a man stroked him with a suede glove, and he fell down.

He fell because he had swallowed too much of the wind, and he died, and they took off his skin and stuffed it – and he became a stuffed exhibit.

Mineral exhibits were placed on museum tables.

There were blocks of iron which had been excavated by Gagarin, the governor of Siberia. He had wanted to get minerals out of the ground, and in Samarkand he had dug up some bronze figures: statues of a minotaur, a goose, an old man and a fat woman. The woman's hands were like hooves, her eyes were bulging and her lips were smiling, and in the hooves she held a candlestick which once had given light, but now did so no more. And in the goose's beak was fashioned a music pipe. And these were gods. And the pipe was there to speak for the god, for the goose. And this was trickery. There were inscriptions scratched on all of them. But no one in the Academy could read them.

There was the stallion Lizeta, which had belonged to the boss himself. Its coat was brown. It had carried the hero at the battle of Poltava, where it was wounded. Its tail was no more than ten vershki[15] long, and its saddle was the normal size. The stirrups were metal and about half a foot from the ground.

There were two dogs, one a male dog, the other a bitch. They had belonged to the boss. The first was Tiran, a Danish breed. Its coat was brown with a white patch on the neck. The second – Lenta – was of an English breed, a normal type of dog. Then there were the puppies, Pirois, Eois, Aeton, and Flegon.

And in the basement there were human items, two heads in jars, in spirit. The first head was that of Villim Ivanovich Mons, and although it had been on a stake for about a month, and been damaged by the wind and the rain, it was still possible to make out that the mouth was proud and pleasing, but the brows were sorrowful. And he was that kind of person, and even at the height of his power, when he was receiving great bribes from every side, when he was sleeping with the boss's wife – he was always solemn. You could tell that at once from his brows.

- Oh, what is the world? All in the world is false.

- I cannot live or die. All in my heart is aching!

Maybe he had not loved the Mistress but only slept with her to get bigger bribes and fortune. And at the same time he was frightened by the risk he was taking, and anticipating misfortune.

And the second head was Hamilton, Marya Danilova Khamentova.

[15]   Sixteen inches

This head, on which the pattern of the veins was so clear, where each vein was going, that the Boss himself, on the scaffold, first kissed the head, and then explained to those surrounding him how many veins went from the head to the neck and back again. And he ordered the head to be preserved in spirit in the Kunstkammer. And earlier he had slept with Marya. And she had many fine clothes and sables and was driven around in an English carriage.

And now these two were looked after by the living freak from the floor above, and he had got used to them. But for the time being they were not put on public display. Because, even though all the veins in the head were clearly visible – it was private matter, and not everyone, even noble figures, should be shown domestic matters.

And in the small chamber there were also some stuffed birds, white, red, blue and yellow. The blue one had a black tail and a white beak.

Who had caught such a bird?

3

The ukaz concerning monsters and freaks: That in every town all deformed humans, farm animals and wild animals and birds should be brought or led to the nearest police post. If they were examined and approved a payment would be made. But few were brought. The widow of a dragoon brought two infants. They were joined at the spine and had two heads each. Whether the payment made was too small, or for some other reason, but in all this great realm there appeared to be no more freaks than this.

And then the Procurator General – Yaguzhinsky – added the suggestion that a scale of payment be created for the deformed, so that it was more just. The tariff was as follows: for human freaks -10 roubles each, for livestock and wild animals- 5 roubles each. And for birds – 3 roubles each. This is for dead ones.

And for living ones: for humans - 100 roubles each, livestock and wild animals – 15, and for malformed birds – 3 each. That people should ignore all rumours that deformities were caused by witchcraft or spells. That the freaks should be delivered to the Kunstkammer. For Science. If someone should fail to deliver or declare then the fine should be ten times what the payment would have been. And if the freak dies then it should be placed in spirit. If there is no spirit then double strength wine would do. And if there is no wine available then it should be placed as it is and a cow's bladder stretched over it – so that it does not spoil.

4

So people began to peer around to see if they could spot any monsters or freaks, because they would get 100 roubles for a human freak. They started to look closely at each other. The chiefs of police and the provincial governors looked especially diligently.

Monsters turned up. Prince Kozlovsky sent a sheep with eight legs, and there was another sheep with three eyes and six legs. He had been riding along a road when he had caught sight of a sheep grazing, and from some angles it looked to have six or eight legs. He was too dazzled by the sun to make out. Thinking that he must have had too much vodka, he continued on his way. Then he gave orders to catch it. The sheep was brought to him. It had eight legs. He gave orders to trace the owner. They went to the man's house. There was no one there. The owner had gone missing, probably most likely hiding in a field of oats. The order was given to take the sheep. Thanks were given for it, and thirty roubles cash. The commandant of Ufa, Bekhmetev, learnt of a calf which had two gigantic legs. But for these legs only 10 roubles was paid. The commandant of Nezhinsk sent a human freak. It was a male child with eyes below its nose, ears below its neck, and the nose itself heaven knows where. Then an artillery-man's widow from Moscow, from Tver street, presented a child with a fishes tail. Then the governor, Prince Kozlovsky went on searching to see if there was a human monster because there seemed to be a great difference between a hundred roubles and fifteen roubles. But there was nothing. Then two small dogs were brought in. The dogs seemed normal ones, except that an old maid of sixty had given birth to them. They wanted two hundred roubles for them, because they were human freaks, nevertheless they were given only twenty, because the dogs weren't even freaks. And an order was issued to all the commandants to scrutinise carefully and then they would get payment. Then the Kunstkammer was sent a pig with a human face – if you looked at it from the side. Its forehead, the pig's, was like a person's, with a human front. But only some people saw the likeness, others did not. Ten roubles was given for it.

Of human live freaks there were three, Yakov, Foma and Stepan. Foma and Stepan were rare freaks, but they were cretins. They were two-fingered: on both their hands and their feet they had only two digits, like claws. But they managed with two. If one offered to shake their hand and said, "how d'you do" then both the freak Foma and the freak Stepan would press your hand and bow. They were both young. One was seventeen, the other fifteen. They were brought in by one of the turnpike guards, and they could not tell you their names or who was who, because they were cretins. Their guard was paid three roubles. Then a master carver of tortoiseshell turned up and said that these cretins were his nephews, and he wanted paying as well. But he was told to clear off because otherwise he would be fined a thousand roubles for not bringing them in in the first place.

The overall guard was an ex-soldier, and often noisily drunk. He would turn up at evening time when there were no visitors, and he would shout out:

"Two fingers! Fall in!"

And the two fingered ones fell in. He did not shout at Yakov. Yakov had six fingers. He had some sense and had been sold by his brother.

5

He was six-fingered, and clever, and had been a peasant. The soil where he lived was worn out and over cultivated. It was all exhausted, but there was a bee-garden, and their father farmed the honey. He had set it up, then died, and stopped being a serf – got out from under the yoke. Then the mother and Yakov, the six-fingered one, became serfs under the yoke. But his brother, Mihalko, was in the army. He had been called up even before the Narva campaign, when Yakov was not under the yoke – he had still not been born. He was fifteen years younger than his brother. And suddenly now, twenty-two years later an order came to the parish – there was billeting, and Yakov was approached by an old soldier who said he was Mihalko. The mother recognised him as such.

He looked strict. When they sat down to table he watched Yakov's mouth to see that he did not eat too much. He had something on his mind. He whistled. He went to the regimental base, and would sometimes go away. He did not like talking. People on the street would shout "Hey, soldier!" after him – and the yoke settled on Yakov.

His mother began to shrivel up, her face turned green, her eyes were hungry, and she also began to watch mouths – to see how much was eaten.

And sometimes she would say:

"Never mind that he used to start shouting and get into fights. So did all the others".

And it was true. The others could kick up a racket. Many had sold their uniforms, spent the money, and began to appear in homespun coats. Five men had gone absent and stopped going to the regimental base. Many had taken wives and set themselves up in homesteads, with their feet in front of the fire. Then they started to tidy up the yard and the vegetable patch. And in a short while the area had expanded and extended on all sides. Even though it caused offence and there were frequent cases of army thieving. All the same, it was possible to live with these rowdy people. And then the regimental base became deserted. The corporal had gone off somewhere, and lush grass began to grow in the yard. Only one sergeant-major was left, and he had begun to trade in grocery and wine, and nothing more was heard about the Balka regiment, nor of Balka himself, the commanding officer.

But Mihalko was busy composing a letter of petition. He knew how to read and write. And then one day he went away and came back. He had spent all the money he had got for his uniform. He had made himself a kaftan out of sackcloth, and sewn his army cuffs and lapels onto the sackcloth. The six-fingered one walked round upset by the look of his brother. He no longer knew his brother. Meanwhile he did his work dues, and worked with his bee-garden, his bees, the honey, and wax. And the soldier ate their bread. Yakov knew how to whiten the wax by moonlight. He had been taught, but the soldier was bringing everything to nothing. One day he sort of thought about this, went outside and looked at the bee-garden. The bee-garden was there in the dark – and he said quietly:

"Don't let that mouth swallow you up."

He went back into the hut and gave the soldier some money to buy wine. The soldier took it from him on account strictly. Yakov's money was hidden in a place even his mother did not know about, actually in two places. One with a small amount in it, the other with more. For the soldier he took from the smaller amount.

Mihalko was composing a petition about his rank. He had already taken two years writing it, a word a day. And he went off to the town and there a clerk corrected this petition for him.

Most gracious Tsar and Majesty

I, your most humble subject, have been serving with all due diligence in the Balk regiment for nearly a year. I received a bullet wound in my back in the battle at Narva. From the wound I got yellow fever for which I got relief at the military spa-baths on the orders of Your Autocratic Majesty. At present I have come to my lowest point in the village of Sivardi. My uniform is old and has holes in it so that people laugh at me when I wear it. I have no character reference or letter of appointment. And at this present moment, in accordance with Your Most Gracious Majesty's ukaz ranks and references are being issued. In reference to which, Most Gracious Sire, I beg your Majesty that I be issued with a character reference. I am prepared to go on a campaign, ready for battle, or to go on guard as a turnpike keeper or watchman, or in an office, so that I receive sustenance.

Your Majesty's most humble servant, soldier in the Balk regiment.

But he was still in no hurry to sign it. He could not remember the year in which he had been enlisted. He had been carrying the letter around under his shirt for six months, and it rustled at night. And the sheets of paper grew tattered, like his uniform. His mother used to wake and lift up her emaciated head, and shake it, as though it were on a pole: there was that rustling noise again. If only he had been noisy.

And then one day his face lightened. He went to the powder store, came home, began to clean his belt, shaved his beard – and his face was beaming.

His mother groaned.

Then he went to Yakov and said:

"You must get ready, on the Tsar's orders, and the command of the Balk regiment. The order is to transport those under arrest to St Petersburg, on the matter of disability."

And he looked round, and his gaze shone like a star. It was directed neither at his mother, nor his brother. He looked everywhere but.

Then the mother and the brother realised that their home was no longer a home, that the bees were only passing through, and it would be for others to melt the wax. What could they do but leave?

So they set off, travelled day and night and spoke not a word. They arrived in St Petersburg, and the soldier sold his brother to the Kunstkammer and received fifty roubles 'on his Majetsy's instructions': soldier of the Balk regiment. And he returned home, and

Yakov became a 'monster' or freak because he had six fingers on each hand and six toes on both feet. And he started to wander round the Kikin house, and he was appointed 'stoker'.

And Yakov looked around at his colleagues. His colleagues were from foreign lands, and they did not move. There were large frogs which were labelled **FROG.**

There was a limpet which could stick to ships and sink them. And Yakov felt respect for the limpet, or as it was otherwise known the 'stickfast', because it was able to sink a ship by sticking to it. He asked the guard, and the guard began to tell him what the exhibits were called: snake, sea-lion, gnat, and Yakov started showing visitors round the chamber. He would take them round the room, pointing with all six fingers, and say briefly:

"Frog. Single spirit"

Or thus:

"Male child. Double spirit".

He was paid two roubles a month. The two cretins received a rouble each. Once, a middle-grade clerk, who had not been given a bread loaf, took hold of the elephant by the trunk. This was strictly forbidden, because if one visitor and then others took hold of the trunk it might come off altogether. Then the clerk started grabbing Yakov's fingers so that he could look and see how the six were growing. At this Yakov, without saying a word, shoved his fist under the clerk's nose, and the latter at once started back. Then he begged Yakov's pardon, and began to show him more respect. And Yakov lived as he pleased. Before leaving home he had gone to a certain secret place, unearthed his money and secreted it in his belt. And this belt Yakov wore all the time. The two-fingered ones were afraid of him, but they showed respect for the guard. He called the two-fingered ones 'no brains'. He would take them into the bathroom to wash. But when he began to look after the two heads in jars in the room below he looked for a long while at Marya Danilovna's eyes.

They were open wide as though she had caught sight of someone she was not expecting. And the freak looked at the structure of her veins. And when he had observed which veins went where then he understood what a human being was.

But most days he was bored, and his boredom seemed to him to come from the elephant which was so grey and big, with a trunk. And he saw the situation; the three of them would live in these rooms until death itself. Then they would become exhibits – natural science.

6

But his brother Mihalko went home without getting a job. He had thought twice about handing in his petition. He decided to wait until a better time. It should not be done unless the time was right. He found big changes when he got home. His mother had taken over the household and was now more talkative. And she also began to look at him in the way Yakov had done. But she could not whiten the wax like Yakov could, and Mihalko could not either. And when the latter arrived home he wrapped up in a cloth the money he had received for Yakov, and pushed the bundle between the stones at the back of the stove. There it was dry.

And the wax was not the same: it had a covering of 'bee-bread' and was dark coloured and kept breaking up. Maybe it had to do with the stove and how it was heated. Or had the bees changed? Where had Yakov learnt how to do it? The wax was all his mother now talked about. She forgot to think about Yakov altogether, but she kept on about how the wax used to be good. All sorts of people passed by their door. Whether they were pilgrims or runaways nobody knew.

And suddenly, one evening, the mother said: all our strength is in the wax. Now the wax is like bread, and wax like this is now appreciated, because the German Tsareva has freckles on her nose, and to get rid of them she eats wax. And this eating wax is white. And the soldier crumbled his bread and felt his letter against his chest. The letter rustled. He banged his fist on the table and shouted, his face white with great fear and pride:

7

The chief warder from the prison and some of the rubbish collectors led them all to the Great Prospect road, took them as far as the turnpike, and said:

"Clear off, and don't come back!"

Then the group of convicts began to shuffle along the roads, like a louse.

The snow was melting and the group slithered about, because they had got out of the habit of walking on solid ground. Just occasionally they had been to beg for food, but then they had been in leg-irons and now they slithered about. There were in the group those who had suffered. They had been tortured. They walked badly. They would go for a while and then sit down, where there was less snow. As night came on they drifted away into the woods and into the villages. The convicts swarmed over the villages as though they were the Neva breaking its banks. They went along the roadways and into the village streets. The villages locked themselves away. There were people wandering about and the guards whirled their rattles:

Click, click, click.

The dogs barked full throatedly, with aggression, their tails curled and their ears pricked.

And here were the soldier and his mother. They were amongst those interrogated. Their stories did not match up at all, so they were interrogated.

The head warder put the mother in shackles, and the mother said:

"I don't remember talking about wax, and I wasn't talking about the tsaritsa, but about that German woman who was with the tsar, but I don't know who she is."

And when she was asked where she had got this subject from, and they gave her two lashes with the whip, she testified:

"He was tall and red-haired and his hair stuck out in all directions. I don't know whether he was a priest or the son of a priest. He was passing through the village, and asked for some water to drink. And he said these things, but who he was I don't know. Maybe he wasn't Russian but one of those Germans."

And they gave the mother five lashes and no more because she began to grow weaker.

They twisted the soldier's arms, and he said:

"The royal person was talked about, and it was said she had freckles on her nose, and she was called a German woman in mean words. And if I have said what I should not you may put me to death. And I am a soldier in the Balk regiment."

He was given ten lashes.

"Fool!" they said to him," There is no Balk regiment any more."

And both gave evidence under torture. And when their evidence was examined to see who was telling the truth it was realised that their stories weren't that different, and neither the mother nor the son changed their evidence. And that the red-haired man would now be extremely difficult to trace because of the passage of time.

But then there was a great change. An order was issued to set everyone free to celebrate many years of good health for the tsar. And the mother and son were set free. The warders took them as far as the city limits, and then said:

"Clear off!"

And the son had chewed up his letter of petition and swallowed it all, so that it should not be found, and even worse befall him. So he had not given in his petition and left St Petersburg as he had arrived – without a job. But the son and the mother did not meet again. They went separate ways and grew weaker. Of what did a pauper's lot consist? Of submission and that no chance should be ignored. A pauper's business is like trading, never mind selling wax on the side. Only now it was not a matter of wax, but getting sustenance, and sweet talking to the young and harsh words to the old men – to show that they were so harmless and downtrodden that they could not even talk properly. They sold low quality goods at the cottages, and got little for them, and their eyes were dull but knowing, and missed nothing that was inside the fences. And their arms had been dislocated nevertheless they shoved into their bag what their eye lighted on. In this kind of way and each by their own route, they made their way back to their home village, and there they met, and without looking at each other, made their way to their home.

There they were met by a smooth haired black dog which began to bark and bare its teeth as though grinding them. Then out of the hut came the village elder's son. He wiped his mouth and asked:

"What do you want?"

And he waved his arm at them:

"Get on your way!"

At that the mother sat down next to a tree and did not get up again.

But the soldier of the Balk regiment looked around and recognised neither the hut nor the people, nor the bee-garden, and he marched off in the direction from whence he had come.

8

The freak beckoned the middle grade clerk with his sixth finger, and said to him: "Here come!"

Behind the elephant, right next to the baby with no skull, they did a deal, and on the following day the clerk brought Yakov a letter of petition. It was long, and written in an old-fashioned manner – and it was seeking release. The clerk was very old and had even worked under the Patriarch Nikon.

Your most humble servant Yakov, son of Shumilin asks you to take note of his leanness, and to also consider that he is now prepared to lose not only his six fingers and toes, but his thin arms and legs, and even his very stomach. Please order that he be not in anatomy, called the Kunstkammer. It is already beginning to make him sick, wretched as he is, to spend every day amongst frogs, drowned babies and elephants. So that he, your humble servant is now become an animal amongst animals, and there is no great learning to be got from him, because he has neither snout nor trunk, nor is his nose below his mouth, but he just has six fingers and toes. And for his freedom he will give five times his price and will spend all his days looking for eight-legged sheep, and finding two-headed calves, or a horse with horns, or a snake with wings, and he will, as required, bring all these to the anatomy, without payment, and by his own transport.

Chapter Three

"Has she sat by the sick bed`
Has she been there to bid her loved-one farewell?"

POPULAR SONG

At half past five a bell began to ring weakly and thinly; the soldier on watch at the Apraksin manufactory was ringing the bell for everyone to go to work. The tocsin also sounded in the powder magazines in Beryozov, on Petersburg Island and ringing was echoing in the wax houses on Vyborg, and the old women were up and off to work in the Spinning Mill.

At half past five it was neither light nor dark, and the snow falling was grey. The lamplighters had already extinguished the wicks in the lamps.

At half past five a bell sounded in his throat and he died.

Chapter Four

"And he not only fights in the cavalry,
but also marches boldly in the infantry"

PASTOR MIKHAIL VALDAISKY

"My heart smoulders, I cannot bear it
I want to have an amour with you"

FROM A THEATRICAL COMEDY

She has had six apart from Nestor

PROVERB

He had been on his feet all day and all night. His gaze was sharp, and on his brow were two wrinkled furrows, as though made by rapier strokes, and he carried a sword, and wore a decoration and the lapels of his uniform stuck out. His walk was like clockwork.

Tick, tock.

His step was precise.

He had lost weight. There was no fat on him. There was only meat left. He was like a bird or a rapier: fly then fly! Transfix then transfix!

And it was just like in the war when he attacked the Swedes: the same sparse woodlands, the same unseen enemies, the same secret commands.

He had asked Yekaterina to give money, and she, without a word, just looked into his face, and opened the State Treasury – here, take. He had kept none of the money for himself, just a small, insignificant sum was set on one side. All of it went to the gentlemen of the Guards. His ministers galloped about day and night. And Minister Volkov came back once and was yellow in the face, galloped in another direction and turned white. And Vyust was always busy somewhere, and his clothes stuck to him with sweat.

And at the necessary time Prince Izhorsky, with his little hand, opened a window to let the light breeze into the palace. Who was lying there in the adjoining chamber? Was he alive? Dead? But he no longer mattered. The question now was - who was it to be? And he let the wind come in. And the wind came in not with the sound of wind, but with a roll of drums. It was the gentlemen of the Guard, drawn up outside. Menshikov's Life Guards. And the gentlemen of the senate, who were seated in the Palace, ceased arguing about who it was to be. They all realised it was settled – it was to be a woman tsar.

Long live Her Majesty, Commander in Chief!

This was the second hour after midnight, and then he realised: that was it! It was all settled! The bird is in the hand!

Then the pressure came off him a little, and he thought it had completely gone, and he went off to wander around.

He started to wander round the palace with his arms clasped behind his back, and he felt more relaxed than before, and began to feel tired.

And at half past five when he went into the adjoining room and the body was still lying there, unattended to – then he felt released from pressure altogether.

And then Danilych recalled from whom he had acquired his civil power, with whom he had exchanged kisses, with whom he had melted down the bells for cannons, with whom he had melted silver dishes for coinage, how much he had appropriated, whom he had deceived. And then just for a moment he became again young Aleksashka, who slept in the same bed as his master. Then his eyes reddened, became wolfish, angry with sadness.

And then Yekaterina began to sob uncontrollably.

And all those who heard this roar were frightened – they knew it was the Mistress. It was necessary to sob noisily. And the whole household started sobbing, and from the street various people could be heard all sobbing away.

And neither the gentlemen of the Guards who were wandering round the palace like a herd of horses in a paddock, scions of the nobility, nor the mousy old men of the senate, nor any of the servants, noticed Monsieur Rastrelli entering the house.

2

He was walking leaning on his cane and breathing heavily. He was hurrying, so as not to be late. In his hand he carried a tradesman's yardstick of the kind used for measuring feather toques or velvet for a dress. In front of him minced his assistant, Legendre, with a bucket containing white plaster, as though he was going to whitewash the walls.

Rastrelli went into the side room, he pulled back the alcove curtain and looked at Peter.

"There's not enough", he said hoarsely and curtly, turning to Legendre, "We'll have to buy some more, and where are we going to get more at this particular time?"

Then he stepped back and looked abstractedly into the distance.

"I told you, m'sieu Legendre," he rasped in a tone of irritation, "that you should spend less time going from osteriya to osteriya, and pay more attention to the business in hand, but you bought too little, and there won't be enough for the legs."

And here he turned to face Yekaterina as she came into the room, and he gave a deep bow, almost to the ground.

"Ah, Mother!" he exclaimed, "Imperatrix! Mighty one! We are making a likeness of the demi-god".

And he suddenly stooped forward and huge tears like peas began to roll down his face.

He rolled up his sleeves.

And half an hour later he came out into the main room carrying a salver with a maquette on it. It had only just set and the master craftsman raised one small, fat finger in the air, and warned that no one should touch the model, or try to kiss it.

But nobody wanted to kiss it.

The plaster regarded them all with the pupils of its protruding eyes. On the forehead there were two wrinkles, one lip was twisted to the left, and the temples were dark with worry and anger.

Then the artist caught sight of something: thrusting and pushing his way through the crowd of senators and gentlemen of the Guards was a short, swarthy looking individual. He was trying to get through, but being prevented, and the master puffed up his lips in self-important pleasure, and his face became like that of a frog, because the swarthy individual was Louis de Caravaque, and this keen artist was late.

Prince Izhorsky tugged at the master's sleeve and indicated with a movement of the head that he should leave, and so the master left the plaster likeness and went out of the room. He took with him in a canvas bag a second likeness, for his own purposes. It was in wax, the legs were plaster, and the insteps and palms of wax.

And the plaster likeness stared at them all.

Then Yekaterina burst out sobbing.

3

He did not go straight home, but drove with Legendre directly to the casting shop. He himself lived in the Liteiny area, opposite the Liteiny Palace, but he did his work next to the shop. He was very fond of this workshop.

It was strongly built, of logs, and a large stove was kept alight in it. There it was warm while all around lay snow, and the Neva was right in front of the workshop.

The workmen were inflating the bellows, as, with rapid steps, and muttering to himself, he tripped past the workplaces:

"Rapota!"[16]

He knew just this one word of Russian, but when he had an interpreter it was no use. He would spit and froth at the mouth, and the interpreter could not keep up to translate. He would dismiss the interpreter and manage with his single word and using his hands. He was understood.

He loved the red, baking light from the stove and the semi-darkness, because in the casting shed the natural light came from overhead from a little tower, and it was a feeble light. And the walls were hollow, rounded and glistened with warmth. Here there were moulds for casting and cannons. They were his work, made of wax, howitzers, little cannons and parts of cannons. Artillery equipment.

He hurried through to the little room he used. It was to one side and in semi-darkness – there was a little window, high up. Here there was a plain table and a bench, and there was a stove as well, a small one, and on shelving around there lay screws and tubes, bomb parts and parts for grenades, and there was a large, flat flagon of rum. In one corner there was a defective cannon, displaying to all how it was not fit for use. It had been cast using the Vinius method.

He placed in one corner the canvas bag containing the head and the shapes, took off his top coat and hung it on a nail, then sat down to work. He laid out on the table some strips of material he took from his pocket and began to copy from them onto large sheets of paper. He wrote out the heading slowly with much scratching of his

[16]   *Rapota is Rastrelli's version of Rabota, the Russian for 'work'*

pen and much pausing to admire his thick writing done with a fine flourish like a bow.

And on the paper he wrote a number of apparently unrelated figures, chaotic shapes, incomplete writing – notes - and clear figures, some small, some large and curvy – the measurements. His handwriting was like a dance of dwarves on the paper, or as though a bush had suddenly sprouted on the page, with flights of the pen, curly pig's tails, hooks. Then a sudden rough pressure, a shrill whistle and a blot. That was what his notes were like, and only he could understand them. And next to a finger he drew a number, and round the finger were gathered more numbers, like a fish with food, and there was a swelling and a wave pattern – and this was a muscle. And a fountain jet streaked out – and this was an outstretched leg. And a lake with a waterfall was the stomach. He loved the splashing of water, and muscles were for him like the splashing of streams of water. Then his pen sobbed across the whole sheet of paper, and he had finished.

And, pushing the paper away slightly, he stared at it, frowning in alarm. And he went on sitting like this, worried. He cast a superstitious glance at the corner where the canvas bag was, containing the face and the parts in plaster and wax. He turned to Legendre with a sigh, and said, as though sorry for himself: "Some warm water."

His assistant poured warm water on the short fingers and looked at them as though they were the most important thing in the world.

"Tomorrow morning have my phaeton got ready, and drive to the wax mill. Get white, only white. In the shop on Gostiniy Ryad have a look for the deepest colours – snake's blood. Spend all that I give you on them, don't let any of it get stuck in your pocket. And I don't want you to show your face in any tavern."

And he looked long and sadly at Legendre, and wondered what other fault he could find with him, and wondered what else he could say that would get through to his assistant, so that he, Legendre, would say what was needed.

"And you will cross Vassilevsky Island, and make sure you make a lot of noise as you are passing de Caravaque's house. You can make a noise urging on the horses, so that de Caravaque looks out of the window of his house to see who is driving past. You may bow to him."

When he heard Count Rastrelli say this Legendre snorted with amusement.

"Why do you laugh?" Rastrelli asked, his nostrils beginning to flare, "Why are you laughing?" he shouted, and then burst out angrily, "I am asking you, Msieu Legendre! I know you! You're always laughing. Get kneading the clay!"

In this he had said the wrong thing, because what was needed now was to warm the wax and make an empty mould, and not knead the clay. That was what he should have said. Then the master began to warm the wax on the stove, and to pinch it. Then for some reason he tasted some on his tongue, and chewed it. The wax did not seem to taste right and he growled:

"This is not Corsican wax, not velvety! Pah!"

The stove was warm and he was breathing quietly. His chest was bare and the hair on it stood on end.

He spat out the wax, rubbed his hands together, and exclaimed joyfully and throatily:

"Plaster! Give me the mould! The right hand! We've started!"

He was already talking to Legendre in a rapid patter without managing to finish his words.

"Snake's blood! Snake's blood from the store tomorrow. Give me the varnish for the coating! Well, what are you standing there for? Plaster!"

And his little hands set to work.

4

The first dream was this: there was a large, pleasant garden, as though it were the Liteiny Sad, and spiky trees, and all the ministers were there, and someone was gently pushing her in the back towards him, towards Levenhold, or towards the other, Sapega. And this one was younger. He had German style whiskers, like spikes, and the sword at his side was narrow and comic-looking.

The second dream was immensely deep, and she submissively sank right to the bottom. And the bottom turned into her youth and the farmstead, and Marta was crossing the farmyard. The moon of Latgal[17] was in the sky and shone down on her bare legs. The dung under her feet was liquid and reddish. She went into the byre to milk the cows. The door to the cowshed was open, and the cows stood chewing and waiting for her. In the middle of the yard was a lamp and its red light shone on her feet and legs. Marta did not go as far as the shed, but stopped by the lamp. All around stood birches with thick, white trunks, their branches quivering, stirred by the wind. And in front of the empty byre stood some girls in a row, their backs turned towards her, the wind lifting their headdresses. They looked like white flags. The girls were singing.

The third dream was simple: a cow lowed in the dream, then it came out of the dream and began to low in the meadow. Marta was anxious, she went out of the house – it was time, time for what, she could not remember. The girls were quietly singing.

And Marta woke up. The girls were still singing. She began to hum along with them.

Where the song came from and who had sung it, she could not remember. She lay there on her own, humming. She could not remember the song, yet sang it quietly.

She could remember nothing.

---

[17] *Latgal is modern day Latvia*

She felt weak and had no strength, and was singing a song she could not remember.

Then overcome by fear because she had woken up as Marta, and not Yekaterina, she swung her legs out of the bed and pressed her hands to her breasts.

She kept getting mixed up in her languages, because some she had tried to forget, and the others she had quickly got used to. And this song and this language came from the time before she was fifteen, and that is where they came from, and that is where they stayed. Near her home there grew a field of green oats, and a willow which leant over touching the water, but still did not fall. The willow stretched out over the water and the children played on it and made it dip into the water. Her legs were the strongest of all. She was afraid of nothing, and jumped up and down. Then she remembered how the teats would squeak when she was milking the cows. Suddenly she wanted to milk the cows, but now she was the Empress and even thinking about such things was shameful. And the language was Latgal and the childhood village was called Vishki. And this village had been lost and forgotten. And a heavy woman, her hair like a strip of felt, her nose red and covered in spots, her bosoms high and white, and she spoke that language – her fostermother. And a grey-faced Latvian, wearing a coarse, grey kaftan, and smoking moss, and silent as moss – was her stepfather. He would talk with the mother late at night and she would listen to them. And their language was the unintelligible Latgal language, sing-song and full of scraping noises. She would watch and listen from a dark corner. Then they took her to a town. And the town was big. In the village they called it Aluksuye, but it was also known as Marienburg, after its castle. It had tiled roofs; the floors in the pastor's house, which she cleaned, kneeling on her knees, were clean. And once the pastor's son started to teach her the German language. He was fair-haired and taught her something altogether different. And this other language Marta understood, and began to speak German so well that the pastor's son could not take it and she was dismissed from her job as scullery-maid. Towards her sixteenth year the town was fortified by the Swedes, by military bands, by troops in smart uniforms, which attracted her greatly. Her skin was nice, in places rough, in other plump with dimples. The local lads used to take her boating on the lake, where on the islands grew lush grass and lime trees, and on one island there was a fortress where supplies were stored, with seven towers. This fortress was guarded by Swedish sentries who would not let boats approach too close, and all the lads with her respected this. The drawbridge was raised like a roadway up into the sky. The windows were lit up at night. Who was in there to light the lamps? And this fort seemed like a whole kingdom, and in the evenings whenever the word 'Swedes' or 'Carolus' came up she had a mental vision of all the seven towers. And she married the neighbour's son, married a Latvian boy – Yanis Kruze. And she became Fru Kruze because Yanis was corporal with the Swedes and wore a dragoon's uniform. Fru Kruze – the dragoon's wife. This young man taught her Swedish, though he did not know it well himself. She guessed what this Swedish language was like, how good it was. And then she came to the notice of a tall man with bushy white whiskers, slim, with a snub nose. His uniform was smooth as a piece of manuscript paper. And he straightway taught her Swedish. And she began to speak it with every nuance because he was a wise chief lieutenant. Afterwards she remembered his name in all the languages, and even when she was already with Vilim Ivanovich she would make a deliberate mistake and exclaim:

Oh, Landstrem!

And then she would laugh and make a kindly gesture: Mons. And once Landstrem came boating on the lake with her. They approached close up to the provisioning fort, and she caught sight of the sentries and saw their faces. Then the sentries saluted, and she flushed with pride. And when the commandant of the whole town caught sight of her in the street, the driest most upright man in the whole town, and he an elderly man whose very name frightened her husband, it sounded like a pistol shot: Vilau von Pilau, he realised who was walking towards him, because she was breathing lightly and walking as though going into battle. And she spent that night with him, and he taught her Swedish courtesies, cunning repliques, because he was already old. Now when she walked along the street all went quiet and the children ran to the windows and their mothers smacked them for looking at her – because the Kruze was walking along the street, because the town had grown too tight around her, like a belt, because the chimneys had become low, and the language of the old women had become alien. As she passed by these old women they said in Swedish, in Latvian and in German one short word that is used to describe women. And Landstrem was an attentive cavalier. He left the town and had talked her into leaving, she had agreed, but then the town was besieged by the Russians, and Buturlin began to fire on them. Then the Swedish language disappeared. The Russians took the town and destroyed the fort and she fell into captivity and the Russian soldiers began seriously to teach her Russian, and she was wearing only a shift, and then she was taught by Sheremetev, and then Danilych himself, Prince Izhorsky. He taught her to speak his way, and he became her boss. And on the first night he left her – for her good conversation – a round gold ducat – two roubles, because her conversation had been good and willing. And she did not talk, she sang. And she listened to all the conversations, all the expressions, and she could use them all, skilfully imitating them, and all of it to get round her boss. She could sense them all by the eyes and by the voice. She knew what the person would be like in conversation. She did not always understand the words, but she pretended to – it would begin in her breathing in her chest, and get as far as her mouth, as a response. And the answer was always clever, always hit the nail on the head. But she understood only one human voice, and that voice was like that of a growing child, the leaves or the straw, or the girls at the farmstead of her youth, as they sang their song.

And she had prepared to go to Kryshborg and Marienburg. How many times had she asked the old man to give her some estate on the Baltic, but he had not done so. And now she went out riding in a gilded demi-chaise, or with a team of eight horses, and guardsmen on light bay horses around her, like chicks round a hen, so that all the townsfolk on the outskirts of the town would come out and bow to her. The catholic priest and the innkeeper, for whom her brother worked in the inn, and the pastor and the courlanders[18] - they would all come out to greet her. And occasionally she would honour

---

[18]   Courlanders = Latvians

someone by spending the night. Then they would all fuss around to please her!

But now they were all dead, and there was no point in going there. Foo! Marienburg! Why go into the depths of the country? To look at the pigs? And the fort was in ruins.

It was indeed time to go, and she realised what was required of her. That she should do something today. She will weep, she will give the guardsmen leave, and pour them wine. She will roll up her sleeves and good luck to them, and she will down a glass herself. But all the same, it's better to do such things after the funeral. They loved her – matushka polkownica[19]. There she sat, expansive, fat, open. Then she was more cautious: perhaps she was being a bit too free and easy? Once it had all been about getting round the boss. Now she herself was boss, and was sitting there quite open. All around was sea, and on other sides forest all round, and few houses. And she could be seen from everywhere, and all the foreign dignitaries were now looking at her. And she had white legs, and she still wanted to travel. She did not understand this diplomatic language. Should she arrange a marriage for Lizaveta with France? But France was dragging its heels, and the delay was because of politics – and because Lizaveta, Lizenka – was a doxy, and besides, already promised. Business, business, Oh! And how were things in the Senate? All about Aleksandr, all about him. But he was so deceitful you could not believe a thing. "Let's go, mother" or "Let's sit down, mother". It had been like that before. How was she his mother? She would put him in his place. It could not go on like that, was not possible. And what had happened twenty years earlier? She had no memory of that. There had been so muc happening over twenty years. And how old he was. Dry and old, like a stick. Pfui! An old man! And she said in Russian the word she had imitated and come to be fond of:

"I am so vexed!"

Then there was a twittering of canaries in their cages. The boss had taken over these birds form Vilim Ivanovich when he had had him executed, and he had hung the canaries in her room to remind her. She pushed her large,red feet into her felt slippers and went to feed the canaries. At that moment she felt unsteady on her legs, as though she were still drunk from the night before. But why? Because it was the start of Shrovetide, and for her it was Shrovetide half and half, and last night had been different because it was considered a holiday. And Yelizaveta –Lizenka, had drunk a lot, and she had not expected that 'Maedel'[20] to be so steady on her feet, and she had taken care of Karl Friedrich Holstein as though he were nothing. What a weakling! Pfui!

If only it had been Vilim Ivanovich with her, that kind and truly loving cavalier! He would have said to her – 'Mein Verderben, mein Tod, mein Lieb und Lust![21] He knew, oh,yes, how well he knew it all! He knew how to travel, whom to receive, what to drink, how to talk, and all the 'Lustigkeiten' – jeden Tag[22].

The cages were hanging over a small table, and on the table were his things. She had ordered them to be brought to her. And the things were really smart, the things of a handsome cavalier, and they still smelt of him. The pipe in a woven gold case. It smelt of light aromatic tobacco, a gilded pouch. She would take it for herself, and carry it on her person. An ostrich feather and a snuff box containing powder for cleaning the teeth. Those teeth, so white when he laughed! A watch with her portrait on the case, done by the artist de Caravaque, which she herself had given him as a present, the portrait showed her with pale cheeks and her head on one side. It was only that her nose was made to look much too big. She brushed the dust from the watch –it was a brand new watch – a beautiful object. And his buttons which she could sew onto a new dress. And the precious stones! How many precious stones she had given him! And the ostrich feather could be stitched to a fan. Yes, he had been elegant, and he always loved show. And the little gold figure with the short sword – it was the god of war. Oh! For he had been such a wise and truly nimble gentleman, and used to write her such songs! Welt, ade![23] The rest she could

---

[20] 'Maedel' - girl (German)
[21] My destiny, my death, my love, my happiness!
[22] Happy things - every day.
[23] Adieu

not remember. And he had died like a common criminal. Now, she would have smothered him in gold. He would have followed her. If he could just have waited two months more, and she herself had almost perished because of him. Pfui! He perished like a fool. He was guilty. He had been careless and boasted all the time. And now he would have followed her, dressed like a doll.

She ordered the god of war to be sent to the Kunstkammer, as a genuine rarity. She put everything in its place, and from that day on forgot about Vilim Ivanovich.

And then, through the twittering of the canaries, she heard behind her the voice of the boss.

"Let's go to Persia!"

The voice was hoarse, deep from smoking, and it was like his voice, an old man's.

And she felt her heart stand still, and the boss roared with laughter:

"Katrina, give me the gun! Ha! Ha! Ha!"

But it was not the boss. It was the boss's Guinea parrot, which had been brought to her chambers when the boss was ill. It had been silent all the while and now started to talk. Wring its neck! Why should people prize such birds and pay such ridiculous sums for them!? And she intended to send it to the Kunstkammer as well, when it pegged out, and the best way of ensuring that it soon did was not to feed it.

It was time, it really was, and she did not lose a moment, but rang her little bell. At once her ladies in waiting came in, and she began the process of washing and rubbing in oil and cream. She was handed a decorated jug in a decorated bowl. And that was something very new, and was fashionable in France. And the jug and the bowl were made of thick paper stuck together, and it held water better than porcelain. And there was water in the jug, and she began to sprinkle this Danish water on her bosom.

This Danish water had been concocted by the apothecary Liphold from nufar water, bean water, cucumber water, lemon water, and the water from bryony and lily flowers. To make it seven white doves, had been caught, killed. The apothecary's assistant had chopped off their heads and plucked them, a little flour was added and into the water. Then it was distilled. She loved this Danish water specially made for her, and she splashed it onto her bosoms with her hand.

But the Venice water which induced a pallor on swarthy skin she poured in anger all over one of the ladies in waiting. This water consisted of milk taken in May from a black cow, and she did not need it, which is what she had already told this lady in waiting before. She was not swarthy, and had her own natural pallor, and she gave a loud shout and poured this water all over the lady in waiting.

Then it all went quickly. She rubbed herself with a pomade of sheep's foot and lilies, for softness and shine, and for something else she rubbed her legs with wax. And, drawing back her ears, she drew on her temple three blue veins in a herringbone pattern, to indicate a headache.

She massaged her right hand with mustard cream.

They dressed her in a black mantilla.

She stood there patiently.

They placed on her head a black and white 'fontange', and arrayed her in a black cloak.

And then, shod, dressed, fat, white, thrusting her breasts in front of her, she went into the reception room.

And she put her left hand, washed in 'angel water', up to her face, slightly covering it, as though in grief – a smell came from the reception room.

And when she entered the room she saw again all the gentlemen foreign ambassadors. The gentlemen foreign ambassadors had gathered here to watch how she wept from ten at night until two midday. And she caught sight of dear Levenhold, young, with his whiskers like arrows, and she knew that she would have him close to her. Then she looked to one side and caught sight of Sapega, her niece's fiancé, still just a boy. And she knew she would have him close to her.

Marta put her right hand up to her face. There, in the coffin, was......
And the tears flowed like heavy rain.

Yekaterina burst out sobbing.

5

He had not been given a position. He had acquired some suspicious looking marks on his body. He was no longer fit to bear arms. He had no 'abschied' or discharge papers. In this state he had made his way back to the town of Peterburk. He was a soldier who had served in the Balk regiment. On the outskirts of the town stood an eating house, in front of which were carved boxes and woven baskets. There were three peasant traders trading there, dealing in wheaten loaves and vodka. He sat down in this eating house to consider things. He had some money, beggings he had collected on the journey. In copper money he had five five kopeck coins, all new money with the state eagle on them, and five dots below the birds. But the old coins and kopecks which had a rider with a pike on them, and deep milled edges. Those no one gave him. Those they hid. Those were thought to have some value. And there were three other coins the soldier tried by biting, and his opinion about them was that they were counterfeit, because the edges were smooth with no milling. Counterfeit coins were also good, but copper counterfeits went for much less than the old ones. That was a loss.

So, as he was trying the coins with his teeth there came into the eating house, strung together, three old blind men. One was fat, red-haired and wearing sackcloth. The second was a man of medium height and the third also. They were led about by a feeble-minded man who kept twitching his head from side to side. He guided them in and sat them down next to each other at a table, and then he stopped twitching, and the old men opened their eyes wide, and it seemed they could all see. They ordered some bread, began drinking tea, and asked for some loaf sugar. They drank noisily, sniffing, and then started to talk. They talked quietly. It was about some ribbons or other, and galoon braid. The second one spoke about wax, and the third said nothing. They started talking again and the soldier heard the words 'magistrate' and 'bailiff', that was all. He could not catch any more, they were speaking so quietly. Then some younger man entered the eating house and bowed to the three old men. And they told the idiot to go away, and the young man joined them, but sat some way apart. Then the soldier went out into the porch. There stood the idiot, still waggling his head, but swallowing great gulps of wine. The soldier gave him some bread to eat and asked him who he belonged to.

"I live with the idiots at the traders' place. And where do you come from?"

"I'm a former soldier in the Balk regiment."

After this the soldier gave the idiot two coins in return for a mouthful of wine. After that they had a chat. The idiot said he was travelling about and dissimulating, and to whom he belonged he had long forgotten, and did not want to remember. He had taken refuge behind this loss of memory, and never talked about it with the traders. They were rich and he led them about to fool people – asking for alms. And the first trader, the fat red-headed one, dealt in haberdashery, the second was also a market trader, and was the first one's brother-in-law, and the third had an interest in a wax or braid factory, and he did not want that anymore, so he had gone into hiding. He also said that they could see better than either him or the soldier, and that they went around like this to avoid the heavy taxes that had been demanded of them. And so they went around like this, linked together, and counted as missing by their friends, registered at the beggars office, and that they had lots of little folk spread around everywhere as agents. And he worked with their other simpletons, and received his food, clothes and some of the money they collected. He was a straightforward beggar simply. He also said that all this had come about only in the recent past – so he had heard from the old men – when He had come under womens' influence and began to poke his nose into boyar monies. But formerly there had been a merchant magistrate, and then traders did not wander off and disappear. At this the soldier of the Balk regiment wanted to shout out 'word' and 'deed', and was already staring at the idiot in amazement, but the idiot asked him:

"Didn't Balk tell you what grows in the forest?"

The soldier wrinkled his brow trying to work out what the idiot should want in a forest. And also trying to remember what Balk had said, but the idiot answered his own question:

"Cudgels grow in the forest!"

Then the soldier changed his mind and did not shout out 'treason'.

"We know all about you soldiers," said the idiot to him, "iron noses and braggarts."

Hearing these words, the soldier of the Balk regiment spread his arms, became more subdued, and replied that he could not serve as he was not really a soldier any more. Even Balk, the officer in charge, had gone off somewhere. His position was lost.

"Give me money", said the idiot, and explained: the soldier would give him all he had, and he would fix him up. The soldier did not give him all the money, but kept the two five kopeck coins back. The idiot explained how to approach the young man who was sitting with the old 'blind' men, and ask for a job in one of the manufactories:

"You say: 'I've heard they are taking on men now for teasing and spinning'. Then you give him your best bow – and now I'm going." And he went into the eating house.

There the old men were resting after their tea, and after the news brought them by the young man, and there was steam coming from their mouths.

"He's disturbed," said one of the old men to the young man in a satisfied tone, about the idiot, "He's wandering in his mind, but he likes his food and eats well, and he walks steadily. That's how we get along."

At this moment the soldier entered the eating house, and the idiot was about to start rolling his head, but the old men said,

"That's enough. Drink your tea. Stop tossing your head like an unbroken horse!"

He drank some tea, bowed, and said to the old men,

"Amen!"

And the old men got into line and went off, led by the idiot.

But the young man remained behind, and the soldier went up to him and gave him his best bow. And the young man took him on to tease and spin, but then when he heard the soldier's military way of speaking, and saw that the soldier was strong, that his hands were hard, and that he was as he was with no trickery – he decided: to appoint the soldier as a guard. To protect the people in the wax factory. To strike the gong in the mornings and to go around with the dogs. The guard team consisted of just four men. He did not ask to see a passport or a letter of release, and simply said, "Alright – with the cats".

The Balk soldier stared at him and then he explained:

"You – fighting the sea lions, and if you don't like that, too bad!"

And they went out into the street.

The barrier at the bridge was already up, and the turnpike guard had already gone home to bed.

The old men were walking linked together in front of the idiot.

The old men were singing:

> "Shem chants a prayer.
>
> Ham sows wheat.
>
> Japhet is in charge.
>
> Death conquers all."

And the idiot was singing loudest of all.

6

"There can be no doubt, m'sieu Legendre, that he was a capable man. But look, such legs! Legs like that should walk and walk and run. They cannot stand, they will fall because there is no support in them.

Don't look for developed muscles in them, fat, smooth muscles, like majestic people have. These are just tendons. They're like horse's legs."

He was not satisfied with the legs, because the legs were thin, and there was no joy in them for his hands. And he went round and about, got upset, and kneaded the wax with his hands. He did not touch the sculpture. Then he looked at the wax in his hand, kneaded a little more, and a gleam came into his eyes. He worked some snake's blood in his hand, and looked again, screwing up his eyes. He warmed it again in front of the open stove. He poked it with some tongs, and drew on the lump something like the shape of a human body. He had the apple shaped ball in his hands. Picking up with his thick fingers a little brush, he coated the apple with spirit, and it glowed from inside, as though freshly picked. And the master's lips pouted like a child's as it reaches the breast, and as if he had formed the apple with his lips and not his fingers.

"The main thing", he said importantly, turning the apple over,"is to have veins. So that there should not be a tendon. So that everything should be full, and no one should think for a moment that is empty inside. Give me some wire."

He fixed the sheets together.

Then his eyes began to flash piercingly, and his lips to chew, and he drew a long mark, hazy with a blue haze, on the cheek with a purely feminine air about it, an apple with little pimples on the skin, sketched with a fine needle, and an exaggeratedly yellow lemon, and a grape, drooping, heavy and limp, fruit of a dark Spanish vine. The grape seemed ready to pop into the mouth of its own accord.

He spread all this out on the defective cannon, and after this turned to Legendre, as a man idle and not wishing to work any more: "have you never heard, m'sieu Legendre, of the emperor Heliogabal?"

"He must be Spanish," said Legendre.

"No. He's Roman. Don't show off your learning, m'sieu Legendre."

At this Legendre adopted an inquisitive and eager to learn expression, and, continuing to mould the join on the instep at the point where it was to meet the ankle, he asked in which century then did this so famous emperor live?

"In which? In the fifth century," the master answered calmly, "Isn't it all the same to you when he lived if you don't know who he was? That's not the point at all. I just wanted to convey to you that this emperor liked fruit like this, and developed them. And everyone was to eat the fruit and drink water, as was the fashion."

And with this he tossed his head, remaining satisfied with Legendre's surprise.

And Legendre said, "Hm! Hm!"

"Wax helps with indigestion," said the master en passant, "and his gentlemen courtiers used to eat wax, and in all likelihood they praised the taste of it, and he himself, of course, ate raw fruit. Such was this Roman emperor." And he poked his finger at the fruits disdainfully, without looking at them. "Such was the dissipation amongst the courtiers," he said to Legendre meaningfully," suum cuique – each to his own."

Legendre smoothed out the instep, and now all was ready, almost. The feet, the hands, and the broad shoulders, the big frame, all lay on the bench. And out of all the parts steel wires poked in all directions.

"Membra disjecta!" the master exclaimed – "legs, feet." And he lapsed into Latin. And this signified that the master would soon slip into a fury. He gave a snort, and Legendre remained silent, but the master said: "You seem to think, m'sieu Legendre, that others have worked out more than me. That maybe, I repeat, other artists can produce a more accurate and faithful piece of work. Is that how it seems to you?"

Legendre wrinkled his nose, neither yes nor no, but on the one hand and on the other, noncommittally.

"Well," said Rastrelli, pursing his lips,"in that case you can go to Caravaque and help him mix up the soot for his paintings. Or, better still, go to m'sieu Conrad Osner in the big shed. He'll show you how to depict Simon Volkhva as a drunkard, flying through the air, head down, and all around him devils turning sumersaults. But just don't ask to come back to me. If you do you'll go flying through the air like Simon Volkhva.[24]" Then he calmed down a little, and said bitterly: "You still don't understand me, monsieur Legendre." Thus he unwittingly honoured him by calling him 'monsieur'.

"You are of course aware, and have doubtless heard of it, in spite of your scatterbrained character – it cannot have escaped you that the

---

[24] *Simon the Heretic*

funeral will be a grand affair. Cornices and architraves, and festoons and thrones. Above the cornices will hang a garland, and on this will be tears embroidered in sequins. Can you imagine anything more silly, m'sieu Legendre? Canopies and clusters and fringes, and Holland and Brabant!"

His nose flared like a conch shell blown by a triton.

"Pyramids, candlesticks, dead heads! In the taste of Marshall Bruce, and General Bok. All they know is marching. The military belching gentlemen. And our well-known Count Yaguzhinsky – that debauchee of all the brothels! It seems he's the main one in charge. He's used to brothels and think they have the best sense of taste – and he's going to decorate the funeral chamber! Have you ever heard, m'sieu Legendre, of statues that pour water as though from a ladle? Oh, you haven't! A weeping Russia with a handkerchief! Mars who is puking with sorrow, Hercules, who like a fool, has lost his staff. Wait! Don't interrupt me! An urn borne by some roaring genies! A washbasin! Twelve spirits carrying a basin. There' been nothing like so many before. Marble skeletons, some kind of drapes. Have you not seen this projected design? Mercy with an enormous backside. Valour with a torn hem, and Concord with a fat belly. He's seen this in some brothel somewhere! And silver heads with wings, and these mugs are also draped with laurel leaves. I am asking you, and I suggest you answer promptly, have you ever seen flying heads with wings and then crowned with wreaths? Where?"

He threw a piece of wax into the stove, and the wax sizzled, flared up, and wept.

"There," said Rastrelli, "it's rubbish! Throw the whole pack away. And after the funeral the honourable ministers will take all these things home, as momentoes, the barbarians, and their young children will scrawl on those large hips various obscene words, as is the custom here on all the walls and fences. And they will fall apart after two weeks. 'Like marble', and in such a case I will express my gratitude. I don't want to make these blocks from artificial limbs. But then, I was not asked to. I cast cannons and create gardens, but I don't want those 'marble' things. And I shall make something else."

With this his gaze strayed from Legendre to the window.

"A rider on a horse. I shall create an object that will stand for one hundred, even two hundred, years. It will still be standing in eighteen hundred and twenty."

He seized the bunch of grapes from the cannon.

"This is what the horse's mane will be like, and the horse's muzzle, and the man's eyes. It was my discovery – the eyes. You are a blockhead, and don't understand anything!"

He ran to the corner, and his nimble fingers drew out of the canvas bag the wax mask.

And what was the meaning of everything he had said earlier – all the unfounded anger over something, all the cursing and snorting?

It all signified superstition – procrastination before the main job.

He still had not touched the face. He had gone around avoiding the canvas bag – this cunning, sharp-witted and speedy artist, and only now did he look closely at the mask, and seemed to sigh deeply and hoarsely:

"The left cheek!"

The left cheek had sunk in.

Was that because earlier on he had taken off the likeness in plaster and had clumsily pressed the dead cheek in which there was already no give? Or was it because the wax had turned out to be too thin? And he began to press a little around the mouth, and was finally satisfied. His face assumed an expression of expectation, and the sunken cheek was not so noticeable.

And so he jumped back and closely examined it, then leapt forward again and put it right.

And he passed a warm finger along the edge of the cut and wiped away the curled lip and the mouth became as it had been in life, proud – the mouth, which is the feature that expresses in the face ideas and learning, and the lips themselves express spiritual virtue. He wiped the sloping forehead, smoothed the muscle on the temple, just as you would in a living person to sooth a headache, and he lightly smoothed the thick vein which stood out in anger. But the forehead did not express love, only obstinacy and insistence on having its own way. And he manipulated the short broad nose a little more and it became sensitive, sensing the achievement of good. The wrinkled ears he made more sharp, the ears which lay pressed close to the temple bone, and they began to express desire and gravity.

And he pressed in the sightless eye, and it became unpleasant like the hole made by a bullet.

After that they mixed the wax with the snake's blood, soaked it and poured it into the mask, and the head grew heavy, as though what had been poured into it was not heated wax, but thoughts.

"No anger," said the master, "or joy or smile." It was said as though the blood was flowing inside him, and he was listening.

And, taking the head in his hand, he gave it the occasional stroke.

Legendre was watching the master and learning. But he was looking more at the master's face than at the wax one. And he recalled the face that the master's face was beginning to resemble. It was the face of Silenus on the fountain, the work of Rastrelli.

That bronze face was one of peace and equanimity, and water flowed continuously from the open mouth. That was the way Rastrelli had exaggeratedly depicted the lascivity of Silenus. And now the master's mouth was open in just the same way. Saliva ran from the sides of his lips, and his eyes glazed over with extreme equanimity and seeming boundless pride.

And he picked up the wax head and looked at it, and suddenly his lower lip trembled, he kissed the head on its pallid lips and wept.

Soon Leblanc brought in the little block. It was empty inside. And the gentleman mechanic with the rank of lieutenant, Botom, brought a mechanism like a wall clock, but without a face. There were little wheels and chains and gears and rods, and he spent a long time installing it in the block of wood.

Legendre smoothed down all the joins, and the likeness was ready in rough. Rastrelli wiped it over with starch so that it should not dry out and crack, and so that there was no dead pollen on it.

And so they placed it in an armchair, and there it sat, but the joins looked like deep wounds, and the torso was leaning back, as though in agony, and the empty eye-sockets showed black.

And because it was a likeness yet not a likeness that was no good for Rastrelli and he threw a green canvas cloth over it, and took a rag and wiped it.

Soon afterwards Yaguzhinsky arrived, already rather corpulent. Yaguzhinsky caught sight of the fruits on the cannon, and wanted these foreign fruits. He bit into an apple and immediately spat it out in surprise.

Afterwards everyone laughed at this curious happening.

On his way out Yaguzhinsky gave instructions that tomorrow, when the eyes were put in, the wax likeness should be sent to the palace to be dressed, and he requested Count Rastrelli to make the silver heads with wings, in return for a large sum, and for them to be flying in laurel wreathes, and also Justice and Mercy to be depicted as female figures.

And the Count agreed.

"I haven't worked in silver for a long time," he said to Legendre, "It is a noble metal.

7

She had been compared to many people. She was compared to Semiramedes of Babylon, Alexandra Maccabee, Irina of Rome, the Empress Savska, Kandakuya of Ethiopia, the two Egyptian Cleopatras, Muaviya of Araby, Dido of Carthage, Milosvata of Spain, of Slavic origin, and the recent Elisabeth of Castille, Mary of Hungary, Wanda of Poland, Margarita of Denmark, Mary and Elizabeth of England, Anna the Venerable, Christiana of Spain, and Eleanor Temira of Russia, and that Kiva, the Persian Emperor, had not only been beaten by her, but had been decapitated, and with the autocrat Olga. And then they went into the adjoining room and they said:

"A good woman, but weak in judgment"

And she did not wait.

Shrovetide that year was a time of gluttony and belly-filling. Everyone observed it. Everyone ate and drank, and she had given them all gifts and food, so that they were all satisfied. From Kiev they had sent her a boar and a Finnish reindeer. The boar was bad-tempered and she gave it to someone else as a gift. And she gave more gifts, four gold tobacco boxes and five made of filigree silver. And although there was a ban on wearing filigree silver, there were not any others, so let them be used. And she tried to do it all according to what she knew people liked. Tolstoi liked gold, Yaguzhinsky liked pictures and portraits and female beauty, naughty girls. The Repnins liked eating, and she offered them everything. She served it to them and ate with them, and made them drink. And she gave so many gifts, and ate so many bliny and drank so much wine and sobbed so much that she put on weight, and swelled up, and in the course of that week she was as though risen with yeast.

And she did not wait.

There in the little palace everything stood waiting, and already the smell itself was spreading round the rooms, and the priests were roaring. Already she was finding it difficult to bear. She felt that her shoulders were free and there was pressure in her breasts, and she felt so light-headed that her lips had begun to droop and her legs to swell with pressure.

Then, at night, she dressed in dark clothes, wrapped a scarf around her, and went whither she needed to. She went past the guards and along the river bank. The snow was melting. It was neither light nor dark. And at the corner he was waiting for her, that young one, Sapega.

They went off somewhere. Her legs moved firmly, and she knew that everything would go well. She was pleased with that. She was not herself any more. The ground beneath her feet had a thin covering of ice. She was not old any more, and not in the least drunk. She walked with a firm tread.

They walked as far as a hut, and he, the young one, began to fuss with the door, but then there was no time, and the ground was not nearly as cold. He spread his cape on the ground for her.

Then she said:

"Ach! That's really good!"

8

And finally he was wept over and laid to rest, and everything was over. In the chambers they opened the windows, and the wind blew through the chambers and freshened up everything. Then they dismantled everything that was there. They took off the belt with the tears, collected Justice and the genies from the urn and sent them off to the Orangery chancelry, to which was attached the Academy for Draughtsmanship.

Then gradually everything was more and more relaxed, and the

Guinea parrot died.

It was immediately dispatched to the Kunstkammer with its cage, together with the gold Mars from Vilim Ivanovich's things.

And then she walked about the chambers as though they were hers, quietly singing to herself.

And it cannot have been a pleasant sight for her in the main chamber: in a high-backed chair, under a canopy sat a wax likeness. And although she had ordered the chairs under a canopy to shut off the alcove with its gilded posts, and to let in between the posts the green and gold sashes, yet everything emanating from him was cold like a vault or somewhere like that, and not homely. He was a 'person' or a 'portrait', but nobody knew how to behave with him, and there were matters no one wanted to discuss in his presence. And although he was actually just a representation, yet he was alike in every detail. He was dressed in formal clothes. She had selected them herself, but not without much thought. They were the same clothes he had worn at their coronation – she wished to remind everyone of this coronation. He was given the best chairs, birchwood ones, the ones that have light stretchers and pointed balusters, in the style current at the time of his pomp, and he sat on a cushion, with his arms resting comfortably on the armrests, as though feeling the galoon braid with his little finger. His camisole was blue and patterned. She had given him a cambric neckerchief, and crimson top stockings, decorated with arrows. His garters were his new braid ones which he had still never tied himself. And the most important thing was that he was wearing, just like a living person, not only all his top clothes as you would expect, but also his underclothes, and the lace cuffs of his shirt protruded. And she could not look away from his feet because they had talked her into having him wear his old lace-up boots, so that everyone could see how much he cared for his country and was economical and not a spendthrift. And the boots, you would see if you looked at them closely, were well worn, the toes were scuffed, the soles were on the point of needing replacing and would soon be ruined. And she could not look too high up, because his head was thrown back, as though in anticipation, and on his head was his own coarse hair, his wig. Neither did she want to look at his waist and his waist belt. His dagger was neither in nor out of his scabbard. She just could not decide one way or the other.

And in his knife pocket were his silver knife and fork: ready for supper! Lunch!

The worst thing was that it could move by mysterious springs in any way one wanted. To begin with she had not wanted to accept it, but to return it to the craftsman who made it, and not to pay him, and that because of the springs they had made, but then it was explained to her that it had been approved by the highest authority. Then she had ordered him to be roped off and tied up, not as a sign of respect, but so that he should not stand up. And she was afraid of getting too close. There was no decent place to keep him. In the house it was unpleasant. There was little happening and he had his head thrown back in anticipation. He sits day and night, in the light and the dark. He sits on his own, and no one knows to what purpose. He made you afraid and stopped you swallowing your food at lunch. It was in no way possible to site him in a workplace because to begin with it would interfere with business, and even if people got used to it it would be bad for morale. And even though it was only a wax likeness, it had the rank of an emperor. It could not stay in the Orangery Chancelry either, where the drawing academy was to be, for one thing because the academy was not yet set up only projected; secondly because it was not only an artwork but also a rare state exhibit.

And so he sat, abandoned by all, but the lesser chamber had been cleared and was needed. As it happened the parrot had died and been sent to the Kunstkammer. Also the state medals with their emblems and battles. And the objects which he had carved – the chandelier, the little plaque, and others – from ivory. These were also important state objects.

And so it became obvious that he should be in the Kunstkammer as an object of special interest for its intricacy, and as a very valuable state object, and a work of art.

That would be his place.

9

Rastrelli had a small supply of white wax left. It lay in a corner in a lump, white, spongy, cold. In the end he got fed up with it. The Master sliced off a fair-sized chunk with a curved knife, and, being miserly, he left a bit to spare. He began to make a model of the monument he wanted to erect in the middle of a spacious square, making it flattering and proud. Now and then whilst working he would assume a dignified air and smile in a self-congratulatory way. The horseman was all of one foot high and rode proudly. Around his torso there were pointed leaves, a glorious laurel wreath. On the rounded base, along the side panels, the master had carved some cupids with open mouths, and dimples on their navels like those girls get on their cheeks when they smile. Amongst the cupids he placed big shells. And then he was satisfied with it.

All of nature greeted our hero with joy and readiness. Savouring past victories our hero rode unhurriedly in his crown of laurels, mounted on a sturdy and handsome steed, and you could see from its muscles that it would go for miles and miles. In fact the whole horseman was less than a foot, made of wax, but it was all a model for the future full-size monument. Besides, it was not clear how it would be received. Would he succeed in persuading them, would they ask him to do it, and how much would they pay? The master said to his assistant, Legendre, appealing to his tender feelings, and boasting:

"They will probably put up a memorial here, m'sieu Legendre. There will be big orders, large sums of money, and much discussion. And if I should die before the casting of the hero, surrounded by my unfinished works, much to the satisfaction of Caravaque, who will, however, peg out long before me, won't he? If I die, I say, from a swollen bladder, or get poisoned by something sent by Caravaque and that scoundrel Osner – I suspect that my cook has been bribed - in such a case, Legendre, you will finish the casting as I shall instruct you, put up the monument properly, and bury me with pomp and circumstance, sparing nothing, with mourning as befits a count and teacher. Any of my money that's left you can take yourself. And all this will make you famous. In no case abandon this project of mine. I'm frightened of dying from a bladder problem. I can feel it coming on. But if I remain alive I shall in all probability increase your salary. And that way you'll get three times the amount than those poor devils who are pupils of Caravaque and that drunkard Osner."

And, softening, the master drank a glass of ale and sent Legendre away. He gave a yawn, took one more look at the model of the proud horseman, covered everything with canvas and summoned the girl who lived with him as a servant, so that she should extinguish his candle and amuse him.

Chapter Five

"She will feel bad, but then you will be calm
You will sleep inconsolably after"

THEATRICAL SPEECH

"Though I go into the gardens or the vineyards
There is not the least comfort in my heart"

YEGOR STOLETOV

He had white teeth, a large mouth, laughed a lot, and the nose of an idler. He had a large house which he had been long in building, he had wanted the house to be square, but one room stuck out and that itself was only half built. If there had been a square it would have stuck out beyond the building line, and that was not allowed.

And in the courtyard he had placed an extremely ornate statue of Flora, carrying flowers in a bowl and smiling. And the women cooks threw the food scraps into this bowl. The house was a palace and round the house in summertime a herdsman from the countryside near the Galernaya pastured cows. He could never get on with things. He was Procurator-General, and he had caught many important thieves. And the herdsman herded and could not herd the cows together. The herdsman blew his horn and the cows lowed. And he waved his hand at all this dismissively.

He made a lot of fuss, and had a loud voice like the twang of a taut cable. He was irritable, almost to apoplexy, and made growling noises in his stomach. He was a coarse man. And right now he was displeased – Pavel Ivanovich Yaguzhinsky.

Danilych, Count Izhorsky, referred to him as 'scum'.

He cursed him as a spoiler, and said about him and his actions that he could put a curse on any business. He called him a bawler and a prima donna, slipshod devil, scum. He said that he played dirty tricks on people, was crooked, fought only those weaker than himself, was a weathervane, a brawler. And he called his house Yaguzhinsky's tavern, because there were all sorts of people living there. And he, Izhorsky, also called it Pashka's Chandelier, as though it were a bawdy house, or a den where wild animals were living, or even women's quarters.

He hinted at this to other people. His woman, Pashka's, was disgraceful. She ran about the houses with her hem hanging down, and he, Pashka, had packed her off to a monastery, while he acquired another woman. A scabby devil and not a lady at all. He said that he butted everyone like a mad cow, that his father had been a herdsman and played a pipe, that he, Pashka, was no mean dancer. He could dance the 'pistol' and the 'grenade', and that he hollered at the gentlemen of the senate. He was a figure of ridicule, a prying person. He called him Mr Farce and also Archduke von Popley. That was a reference to him being a man of feelings, and that he liked sensuality and music, that he was familiar with actresses. He engaged actors and liked dramatic activities, and Mr Farce and Archduke von Popley were the latest drama titles. And maybe it was because he was good at speaking foreign languages and liked to show off in front of other people: Farson. Or that he was only a count and wanted to be a duke, but the pot was already full. Archduke von Popley. That he poked his nose into things and was an informer. In saying this he was alluding to Pashka's appointment. Yaguzhinsky was a colonel and a major-general, but most importantly he was 'the eye of the state'.

This eye watched and the nose pryed into everything, and sniffed out things and altered them. He feared nothing, because he was a roisterer and a bawler.

He was a vulgar man, and entertained no one. He crept about and sniffed things out. Nobody got the better of him. He could not be bested. It was only nowadays that he drank too much, home-brew, wine, English ale beer, now he downed all this greedily. If he could not get wine now he would weep. Because he was alone. And whenever something came up he would stop it and be ready for action, so that he could set up snooping, observation, getting the business under way to see who should be punished. And if anyone tried to touch him then the Yaguzhinsky throat would open, the eyes would bulge, and there would be a throaty roar:

"Ho – Ho –Ho –Ho!"

People feared this threatening roar and the very glass in the windows shook from it. But he got over it, however displeased he was.

He had said earlier about Danilych, Mr Oranienbaumsky:

"Human crap! Greedbag! Dog's paw! He has a crowned heart in his coat of arms, but the mice have eaten his own heart! Dead wood! He does bad things to the people below him, and those above him he publicly flatters. It's all the same to him if the state loses out. He just wants to sneak into the nobility. Prince Kushimen! He's got the whole of Russian Europe in his pocket. He crosses them all, whether he knows them or not. Stingy, devilish counsellor of Achitophel! Overweening Goliath!

And here he was alluding to the nightly conversations between Aleksandr Danilych and his sister-in-law.

"And what does he want with Barbara, when he's already got everything in his pocket?!"

And Danilych, hearing of these sweeping insulting remarks, used one short word to describe Yaguzhinsky: "Zyuzya![25]"

But now, when Yaguzhinsky was on his high horse fulminating, he had not been toppled or exiled, he would lock himself in his room at evenings. And he would sit alone. Now his wife rarely showed herself there. He had a clever wife, marked by smallpox as though chickens had been walking over her face. He did not like looking at her face. He preferred to see her from the side or from behind, so that he could not see her face at all. Now he'd even stopped looking at her from the side. Now he was thinking.

---

[25] *Drunken sot*

He was counting on his fingers: Osterman – self-indulger, silent dog – it was not clear whose leg he would bite. Arapsky – gluttonous, not willing to do anything. Thief. Mr Bruce – neither fish nor fowl. A man of the middle ground. Then the gentlemen of the guard, parasites, war without fighting. And then who? And then who was there? Then the throng of the nobles – the Golytsyns, the Dolgorukovs, -tartar soup – boyar[26] froth. So now he was alone, Pasha, Pavel Ivanovich. And he was not afraid, he was just very sorry for himself, almost to the point of crying. He gave a wheeze, and drank some ale-beer. Then he ordered the Swedish prisoner, Gustafson, to be brought to him. Gustafson lived in his house for various reasons: for music. He would play for him in the evenings when there was partying going on. He would play on the piccolo. And the sound of the piccolo was sweet and torturing. It drew tears from his eyes and seemed to bind him with a rope. So he tortured himself because he had sensitivity and emotion and not simply a great roar and a holler, as some people said about him. Gustafson played to him. Pavel Ivanovich sipped an infusion and looked up at the ceilings. They were stucco, but in the German fashion, and in the very middle the artist Pil'man had depicted for him a naked woman standing amongst some flowers, and as a joke Pavel Ivanovich had got him to sketch on the right the figure of a well-known actor, and it had come out a good likeness.

Pavel Ivanovich next looked at the woman's stomach, and then at the walls with the Indian hangings, and these hangings had already in places been shot through, torn and spattered, for fun. He ate a lot. The food was a gift from various embassies – from the Viennese – metwurst, and from the Danish – anchovies and smoked herrings from a little barrel. As he was now drinking a lot of wine he ate randomly, both Viennese and Danish, threw the bones under the table, and listened to music. The sound of the pipe was so thin and rounded, like a girl's voice, a human voice which all the time expressed different feelings. It fussed and fidgeted, wept, twisted like an awl, grew shrill, almost to a whistle, and then grew full again, and then it seemed as though there were a third person in the room, another person, not the Swede, Gustafson. When the Swede had played his torturing music until the tears flowed, Pavel Ivanovich suddenly

[26] *Nobleman*

stopped him and sent him away. He suddenly thought that, oh, how good it would be if he were the chief counsellor, and not Danilych. That really would be good. And then he began to calculate again: Apraksin – glutton, thief, and the others, and then, whether from the infusion or the music, he came to the thought: after all, at this very moment Danilych is probably sitting on his Vassilevsky Island and also calculating. And who did he reckon in addition? All the regular ones and he himself, Pavel Ivanovich into the bargain. And who will Danilych stop at? Because he had to stop at someone. And he would go into the boyar clan. And if he goes there he will bring back from Siberia Shafirov, Shayushkin's son. He is married to Dolgorukova, and he will win over all the boyars. And if Shayushkin's son comes back, then Pasha Mishin will lose the island which had been gifted to him when it was taken away from Shayushkin. Three cottages! The sea! A grove of birch trees!

Let not Shayushkin's son together with Aleksashka become Tsars! It would be alright if they had been merchants, council people, but they were artisans, common people even!

"Ho, ho, ho,ho!"

Then the real rumpus started.

2

They took him to the Kunstkammer at night, so that there were no rumours or talk. They placed the box with all the equipment in the carts, covered with straw, and took it off to the Kikin palace. The soldiers rode in the dark – they were carrying something – it could have been forage - it was of no concern to anyone.

The guards carried it all in, and the two-fingered ones helped. They were still half asleep – the dawn had not yet broken, and what kind of help were they anyhow? They lighted the way. In their claws they held the biggest candles to be found in the Kikin quarters, and tried not to let them get blown out in the wind.

And in the chambers they cleared a big space in a corner, moved the reindeer to one side and changed the siting of three cupboards. For two days they hung drapes there and put together some steps which they covered in scarlet covers with braid, and they draped it all in red damask to keep the dust off. They put up Leblanc's creation with a laurel branch and a palm. On the tester was a wooden pillow, fluffed up with folds, as though it had just been taken from a bed. That was how Leblanc had fashioned it. On the pillow was the Tsar's imperial crown, and above the pillow, standing on one leg, was the state bird, the eagle, as though frozen in movement, or about to fly, in its beak a laurel branch and in its claws the letters P and P.

When they were erecting it they broke off the laurel branch and one wing. Leblanc repaired it, varnished it , and was paid extra for the repair. For the drapes and the block of the main work he received a not inconsiderable sum, and was now preparing to leave the city.

They even lifted the floors and Botom, the mechanic, installed under the boards various cogs and wheels – the underfloor equipment.

They sat him down. He was facing the window. And on either side of him they placed a cupboard containing various of his own clothes. And up in the window they hung the Guinea parrot, and in one corner they placed his little dogs, Tiran, Eois and Lizet Danilovna. That was what he had called her, and this Lizet was as though the blood sister of Danilych. That was what he used to say as he joked and laughed. She was a ginger coloured dog, of an English breed.

And in the corner was a horse, also an English breed, but she had grown mangy, so that they had covered her with a horse blanket, which also had the letters P and P on it.

But subsequently they had second thoughts. The dogs did not matter. Dogs were not only allowed indoors, especially by German people, but bones were also thrown to them like well-educated people do. And if dogs were trained they even carried things between their teeth, showed how clever they were and entertained people. But only Caligula, the roman emperor, allowed horses indoors, and he was a lone example of quality. An important showpiece should not be turned into a horse stable. Even though it was his favourite horse, and had taken part in the battle of Poltava, yet it was mangy and smelt of decay. So they soon removed the horse, and the horse blanket.

And while they were dragging and transferring some of the exhibits they re-mounted them, and there drifted out of some of the jars a vague smell of spirit. And that night the six-fingered one walked through the portrait chamber – that is what they had started to call it.

It was dark. The guards were asleep. They had been overcome by the fumes from the jars. He could see the three dogs, Tiran, Lizet and Eois, and the dead fur on them was standing on end.

And there, head thrown back, dressed in blue, arms resting on the armrests, long legs stretched out comfortably in front of him, sat the waxwork.

The six-fingered one gazed at him from a distance.

So that is what he was like!

Big, wearing a silver star!

And he was all wax.

All his life he had gathered wax from the hives in the bee-garden. He would heat it, cut it, and work it in his hands – sometimes he would make candles of it. His fingers knew more of wax than of the bread he had eaten that day. And it was from that wax that they had made a person.

What for? Who for? Why had this person been made, with the dogs standing there, and the parrot hanging there? And this person looking out of the window? It was dressed, shod, and its eyes were open. And he wanted to feel the wax with his fingers. He stepped even closer.

Then there was a muffled grinding and clicking sound, and the figure began to stand up.

The six-fingered one stood like the exhibits stood in the corner – not breathing.

And it squeaked and whirred, like a clock before it strikes. Then, shaking slightly and standing at full height, turning, the waxwork gestured as though beckoning and saying to the six-fingered one: Greetings!

3

That month there was a lot of entertaining and drinking of wine. When people met together it did not seem so strange to them that all around was bog and the air was foul. By then that fear had passed. People had become more polished like stones in water, and become incapable of stubbornness and contrary opinion, and there were sledges, all sorts of wide ones, and when the snow had gone there were carriages as well as coaches, and they rattled round the city. And most people travelled in short carriages, so as not to have to take accompanying lackeys, and only two servants, so there should be no extra show.

Over the course of today Pavel Ivanych had been at the Ostermans', and at several other people's houses. And in the evening he entertained people of lower status, merchants, then former members of the council. His guests sat with him in the room where on the ceiling was the faithful painting of the actress's stomach – Myakinin Aleksei.

Then they all left, and he went over to the window and saw: on the other side of the Neva there were lights in Menshikov's cottages. All was peaceful and nothing was happening, no big fires or floods. Everything was in its place, and where Menshikov's house itself stood was not visible from where he was standing. He then began to wander from one mirror to another, and all the mirrors showed one and the same thing: his lips were drooping, his eyes were filmy from the infusion. His nostrils were flared, and he was muttering all the time through his white teeth – puffing and wheezing. Then he smacked his lips, his thick voice, varying between the grinding of teeth and an animal moo. And at the end of what he said there was snorting like bitter laughter. Altogether it was as though he was learning or rehearsing a comedy, a new one that no one had ever heard. He sidled up to the mirror next to the door – it reflected the right hand window into the courtyard – and said in a whisper:

"Mohammed's dragon!"

He looked around himself with a knowing and savage look, and saw nothing apart from the furniture and the silver. Then he spread his hands as though in full and final incomprehension, or as though he had done everything he could, and could not be responsible for anything else:

"Goliath!"

And, giving a sigh as he walked to it, he looked out of the window and caught sight of a lamp, and the lamplight which fell, as it seemed, like a curving fountain through the window panes and onto the ground. He had had it placed there at his own expense, on a metal pole, as an example to others.

"Lamp money?" he said threateningly.

And at this he screwed up his eyes.

"And why, gentlemen of the senate – although it be only lamp money – why, from Admiralty Island all along the Moika are they collecting money kopeck by kopeck?"

"Isn't it because," and he raised his finger in the air like a Roman orator, "Isn't it because Menshikov's son-in-law lives there? And there's no money in St Petersburg?"

He gave a bitter laugh.

"And if the lights are not shining, and they aren't, why have additional collections been made? Square money, bread money, bathouse money, straw money, firewood money, both for cut down and fallen, and ring money, bitter money." And he reached for his lapel as though giving a sob.

" I live for taxing – and not for governing. I ask, and I even order, but I always get a hard answer!"

And, letting out a breath, he began to count off briefly and rapidly: "Runaways, the dead, those taken as soldiers, not excluded from the poll tax, and those running away to join the Bashkirs…."

At this point he drew his finger across his right temple, because he had forgotten something. He took a few steps, then hesitated, and pointed at the window, straight at Flora carrying the flowers.

His pock-marked woman came in.

And the pock-marked one sat down and began to listen, and he said to her instead of to Flora:

"I tell you, Anna, and I declare that after the disposition of the regiments to their quarters there has been a loss of serfs. They advanced into the kingdom of Kazan, and now there is a shortfall of thirteen thousand human souls. That's a really careless shortfall, isn't it?"

The pock-marked one, eyes downcast, listened and fluttered her eyelashes. She was clever.

"Because I am telling the truth," he said to the pock-marked one – though the latter did not respond, "though it wasn't without horror that I heard that one woman was driven by hunger to drown her daughter by throwing her into the river."

The pock-marked one just wanted him to go on talking. The woman did not matter to her at all. Neither did it matter to him. But then he got angry with her for her lack of feeling, and he rapped on the table.

"From the gentlemen officers we should increase the amount by half. Because we are at peace. And let them come from Peterburk, and put their sword back in its box for the duration. Or they should be fighting – and not with women!"

And with this he poured out and downed an ale-beer, while the pock-marked one said:

"And the Persian business…"

Without finishing his drink he waved his hand at her, and asked:

"And why was it the soldiers were taken off their work on the canals? The canals have also fallen into disrepair. What for? And work will stop on the Petersburk column of course."

And, tossing his head back in haughty anger, he gave a crafty smile.

"but there will be no revision now, gentlemen of the senate! Nothing will be revised because that far-sighted princely mind does not permit revisions. It can see things anyhow.

And he spread the palms of his hands like fans before his eyes in a mocking way, and spilt the ale-beer. And with that he threw the glass on the ground with a crash and a tinkle.

In commerce the world over this is the general basis. And for the tariffs he puts the bribes into his own pocket. Not without fear! And now the people in commerce are bewildered: should they transfer their business to the Archangel area, or should they transfer to Kronstadt? Or should they withdraw altogether? And should it be St Petersurg or the City? "Give me an answer, gentlemen of the Supreme Senate," he said to the pock-marked one, "because it is a problem of some significance, and Petersburk is already under threat."

"The Danish business," said the pock-marked one quietly, and shook her head in considerable alarm and fear, but approvingly.

"And I watch with considerable horror and fear," and he took her hand in his big red paw," at how blind is Her Highness's war machine. What savagery! It has thrown its weapons on the ground, and its officers have already been turned into house-lackeys! It gets what it wants by force!"

Running back into the middle of the room, and tearing his kaftan open at the chest, and turning his head from side to side, he roared out: "and everyone's coming to me and asking for justice! What power do I have? No comfort and no joy! And blood will show the way!"

The pock-marked one flickered her eyelids very quickly.

But he went on turning his head from side to side, as though searching for some object or for additional words, and suddenly, unexpectedly even for himself, he roared out:

"Goliath!"

With this he collapsed into a chair and looked around: the candles were burning, reflecting on the silver, and there was a spot reflected on the wall. The chamber was big, and could have been made smaller. In one of the chairs sat his wife, pock-marked and astute, and there could have been another sitting there, not so astute, but not pock-marked. And still she did not leave her place and around them the city had become fluid, and might empty out as summer came on. It would tremble and creep along. What a city! Thirty thousand human souls, and already creeping outwards. The area facing the cottages had been fenced off. That was where the master shoemaker, the German Mikhailo Grigor'ev, had lived. And where had he gone? Disappeared. They would wander off from where they worked, and would say the site was too boggy. But tomorrow he would frighten them, as he would frighten a dog with a stick.

That was enough for today.

He said, after a silence, and in a quite different tone of voice, as though with longing and sorrow in his heart:

"Tolstoi has promised and Osterman will stay silent. And, Annushka, for tomorrow you can get my sash ready. And I've got enough ale-beer in for tomorrow. Send in Bardens. And please call the barber and he can let my blood."

4

Since his childhood the chamber he remembered had been small and low-ceilinged. The walls were soot-stained and the wood smelt of smoke. The space in the room was taken up by a stove, and on the stove was wood.

In the middle stood a huge cut slice of wood, as though an oak were growing in the room. It had been felled and this was the stump.

His father was fat and red in the face, and his sweat dropped onto the sheets of dough. He emptied out a large pan onto the wood stump, counted out loud, and when he reached 'forty times forty!' he stopped counting, wiped away the sweat from his forehead with one finger, wiped his hands on his apron, and baked no more. The apron was reddened, scorched, and stuck out. His sharp-nosed mother rolled the dough so thin on the stump with her fingers, as though she were a seamstress and spiced the dough with onion and sheep's heart.

He, Aleksandr Ivanovich, could still smell the thin pervasive smoke and the pitch. His father would say little, would leave the house and would come home noisily, no word spoken, with no trousers on. But his mother was sharp-witted and would be sitting in one corner, counting the money. And when, many years later, he was at sea, and was already an admiral, he once again smelt pitch. The sailors were caulking the heads, and the smoke was sweet, the very boards had been sweetened by the smoke. Then, for a short while, everything was brought back to his memory by the smoke: the little room and that stump and his father, the red back of his neck, the stove, and: "Forty times forty!"

He had recalled these things on three occasions in the past years. And then he had ceased to recall them because he no longer remembered. He lived without memory, and everyone around him could see how he had changed. He had changed several times in his life. Once he had been slim and quick of movement and very good-looking, mischievous, busy and eager. And you could see that he had no desire whatever for long-term self advancement, but instead there was just a lot of movement, excitement and laughter. Then for five years he had walked and ridden about, thick-set, well ordered, circumspect with people and eager. Then he got carried away again, became cunning, turned away from people. His face grew ugly and red veins stood out on his sharp nose, and then he began to grow away from his beginnings. He forgot about who he was and distant thoughts came to him. His eyes grew focussed. There was a restlessness and people became all the same to him, there remained only his sons and his daughters. He still thought of them and was aware that they were his blood.

He had become 'elevated'.

He sat and looked at his excellent stoves, looked at the palaces, the ceiling papers, fine carving, and it all seemed to him alien, cold. Perhaps he should build a new palace or travel somewhere? He would take his snuff box in his hands and sniff the smell of tobacco from it – earlier it had been that his fingers understood this snuffbox. They knew that it was his, where the corner had been rubbed – that this was time, and that this was his thing, his chattel. His nose cleared, and clear memory appeared again. He knew what he had to say that day, and what comical happenings there had been the night before. That the fool of a cook had bitten his backside, that there were more things to do tomorrow, and that the day was over.

And now the day was not over. In his wide-ranging and distant thoughts he took his snuff box in his hands and put the snuff up his nose and forgot what he was holding in his hands. His fingers got hold of the tobacco as though plucking it from the air, and it was all the same to him – he had ceased to value objects. A lot of new snuff boxes had appeared – gold filigree, one with a pearl, another with a diamond – and he had lost them. And there got to be more objects, and less good – many precious metal objects, expensive and in the new style, but as yellow as copper. And now when he was talking to Varvara he began to twist things, because he could not tell her everything, and formerly she knew about all important business. Her bedroom was right next door. When he woke up at night he was surprised himself at how veiny and taut he had become, like a bow string.

And there was business and losses. The town of Baturin, which he had once taken by storm, and naturally, laid waste to, a possession in perpetuity, he had to govern one thousand three hundred households and altogether under him there were a hundred and five thousand human serfs, not counting the landed estates in Pochepsk and Poland. And for the losses in Ingermanland he had been granted forty-five thousand serfs, and for cash an inviolate sixteen thousand. And he had asked for little – it could have been thirty, and this was a loss.

And what was his title now? Prince, or if you like Count Izhorsky, or Prince of Rome, with ostrich feathers in his coat of arms and his princely hat? And he wanted to be like the Prince d'Artois in France. But at the same time that was against all the Tsar's practice, and would always be that way, to be called Generalissimo, or if that wasn't acceptable, then – Commander General of Russia.

In the day he did many things and used words he had forgotten for twenty years, with Katerina.

He knew how to charm her day after day.

To begin with, pointing at the coffin, he said:

"Mother! Highness!"

And then, in another room:

"You don't say much about business, mother!"

And he already pronounced this 'mother' in a different way.

And then, day after day, he once again trained her to nudge things forward, to reach with her hands, to get nearer.

And when they took it away and buried him, then he showed up.

He could be savage in these conversations, and so at times, when he could think of nothing, he could still see her as Katerina. Then it seemed as though a wheel started to go round in his head, and it was a wheel he could not stop.

'I want to be formal regent, so that it is my job alone to rule!'

And so it went on – me, me, me, just me!

He did not want to be regent at all, but rather Generalissimus, but he did not want to elevate himself, he got on with things. And she was still all too obvious, and this spun round and round in his head.

He kept forgetting all this, and could not even stop and think what he had to do for this the following day, and he did not think, but acted next day and without any such thoughts – again when he was with Katerina and looked sharply at her – and her eyes were closed. Then again the wheel would start, and by then something else: 'marry the princess to my son, and then, then he would be regent.'

And then he would put it to the back of his mind, and act accordingly on the following day.

And then items grew less or not less (there were more and more items) – but everything around became bare. Just like on a ship when it is already out on the open sea – things on it change. The very dishes, whether porcelain or pottery – and the benches, all become strange. And when they come into port objects on the ships change again. They are time-limited, temporary. They become different objects. And he began to understand himself – how that from the side he was lean. And he began to realise that his voice was dry and without the inner softness that it used to possess.

And once when he was carried away and she, Katerina, lay full length, he realised that she had grown old, and he did not think, but simply said something like:

"How can you get rid of a person? How to get rid of her, how?"

And he even murmured this because at that moment he was not without desire for her, for Katya, and there was no way he wanted to be rid of her at that particular time.

And then another change had come about: he became more cautious with people, and although he was angry and spiteful, yet after the angry outburst, if the other person bowed low, and was humble, he also favoured him with a bow. He even began to forget wrongs done to him because he had not seen people as people. And he had stopped making fun, as people had always previously seemed so amusing to him. Thus had his position of power affected him.

He summoned his enemy Shafirov back from Siberia, and he considered his ministers, messrs. Volkov and Vyust, and thought with some severity:

"They're thieves."

He began to be afraid of the big bribe he was offered, because all the bribes at the moment were small. And the others, undoubtedly, were also taking them, and wasn't too much capital leeching away? There was disorder amongst his lifeguards. Vyust was not above suspicion - red-faced, forever taking bribes, a venal man. And now he was building such grand stables, and he gave off a delicate smell – that of scented Maieran grass. Oh, how he will take bribes, and how much interest!? That was what was of not insignificant interest.

And he decided that later, when he was confirmed in office, he would get rid of Vyust. He would give him a testimonial that was reassuring, and off he would go.

And he looked at his daughters with an experienced eye, looked at the whiteness of their skin, at their bosoms – how would they develop? He looked at them carefully, selected and made his choice, and he chose Marya. At times he admired her, and his wife he stopped seeing, as though she were a stray and had got separated from the herd and somehow made her way into the house.

And before going to the Senate he felt uneasy, he had to make things better for people. He summoned his minister, Volkov. After that night when the throne changed hands Volkov had begun to waste away, to go yellow and breathe heavily. He was angry with Volkov. There had been a lot to do. He had been there and he had caught a cold – that was fair enough – but to look so bad, and that as though on purpose, and to be pitiful to look at – that was becoming boring. He, Volkov, had been given money and land, all for that night, so what was he doing catching a cold?

Count Izhorsky said to the minister:

"Have you prepared the ukaz about relief in the tobacco trade? And about nostrils?"

At this Volkov thrust into his hand two sheets of paper. The Count took these two sheets carefully in his hand, and gave the contents a cursory glance.

He understood these sheets printed in the new alphabet and knew how to hold them, which way up, because they always started with a capital letter. There were also other marks: below the line of printed characters, to stop mistakes being made, a word had been placed which then came first on the following page, and from this isolated word one could tell whether it was the top or the bottom of the page.

But here he had been given a manuscript which was so evenly written, without tildes or tails below like chaff. And the minister, Volkov, looked at it dolefully. The noble eyes read hesitantly through the papers, from one sheet to the other, and his hands were holding these papers upside down.

"It's making my eyes ache," said the count, "they're waiting for me in the Senate."

Volkov pointed his finger at the paper, from the bottom to the top:

"It's an abstract of the tobacco trade regulations and the decrees which used to be there under the previous tsar. And the earlier files about the slitting of nostrils."

Prince Aleksandr looked up at the yellow face, so boring it would make you yawn.

"Don't bring me dead papers," he said," that's enough. Let the nostril ukaz be effective from today. The nostrils should be split to the bone. And as concerns the tobacco business, simple tobacco, both twists and flakes, let them be sold without duty. This should be proclaimed to the drum beat all through the city and along the river Moika. And through the settlements."

5

And the city stood there, and suddenly the snow began to melt. And people were going about the streets, and the streets were steaming a lot because they were unpaved. They had not yet been trodden flat by peoples' feet. Only little paths had so far been trodden smooth at the sides, and they showed at the end of the streets and the hummocks. Round the Nevsky prospect street the bog was sweating heavily. In the morning there was a smoky mist as though everything was burning, but there were no fires. People in Petersburg talked about this at the time – why did the bog sweat and steam so much? And the firewood situation was better, because it had begun to get warmer. More and more people were coming to the gypsy encampment, to the evening throng. They went there for the warmth.

In the Gostinyi Ryad[27] arcade there was a brisk daytime trade, and in the Tartar settlement, the burnt area, there was evening trade. Here there was excited shoving and pushing. And trade loved places

[27]   *Street consisting of accommodation for noble visitors*

like this. Even at the bastions stalls had been set up twenty years ago, and there business was sluggish and the booths were new. A bridle had been hung up, or a trader's apron – strictly organised trade, little shouting and no sign of mud. Then the rows got burnt, and how they came to burn was a murky, devious matter. Burnt huts began to appear, made of burnt planks. Tartars turned up – old clothes dealers, there was an Armenian with Armenian goods, thin faced. Then in one secluded corner a half drunk artisan set up a booth for drawing teeth. He was a Swedish or German man, and was already known to everyone in St Petersburg. And all around there was shouting, then silence, and then – Ow! – and a tooth was drawn. He also sold apothecary goods, with the bottles arranged right there on the ground. If asked he would come to your house to let blood or cut hair, because he also had blood-letting equipment. He was a barber. There were lots of people there. Passageways had formed around the trading booths and the corner sites, various tradespeople, holes and ditches. Rubbish accumulated. There was shouting , oaths and simple gawping. Thieving was rife. Already a blue kaftan[28] would be chasing after someone, and unslinging their flintlock rifle, and shouting out – Thief! The air grew thick with people.

And it began to get muddy. The area became cluttered. There was mud underfoot, on the stalls and on peoples' hands. There were various kinds of mud – Kalmuk, dry rubbish – from the horse equipment, tartar rags from the old clothes stalls, and fat and meat dirt from entrails and carrion – and this was forbidden by order of the chief of police. It was forbidden to sell slaughtered meat which had not been butchered, offal should be cleared away, and meat traders must all be dressed in white, for greater cleanliness. The fine for non-compliance was three roubles, and other offences had punishments such as flogging with the cat o'nine tails, and hard labour. But these were rarely enforced. And there in this little square was a row referred to as the scent row. It gave off a smell of perfume. There the scales were not approved ones, the containers were not measured, and the livestock was all deadstock. And there livestock was passed or dragged from hand to hand, and there were shouts of:

---

[28]   Police uniform

'Hey! Don't damage the goods!'

Here, next to a tub, stood a merchant selling kvass to all comers.

Pie sellers shouted their wares. The pies were wrapped in cloths like babies at the breast. The cloths were worn, but there was warmth in them, and that also cost a bit of money. Cold pies were cheaper. And next to them was a Finnish peasant from their village beyond the island, and he had containers with salt. He was a rich peasant, and those wanting to buy dipped their finger into the salt and then licked it. And then they would look at it. Other people would watch the customer. He was trying the goods. Then his eyes would widen in a troubled way, as though this was the first time he had seen such a sky, and such a city, and crowded rows of stalls, and the Tartar camp. And once more he dipped his finger more deeply into the tub and put it into his mouth. And everyone watched how he looked at the goods. He made slow movements with his tongue, and something was going on there inside his mouth, and then stopped. He shook his head:

"Not good!"

And with that he was gone. He went off into the crowd. He was trading in horse tack.

Then suddenly he would turn up selling old trousers.

There were all sorts of people. Trading people and sellers of bric a brac. They were not fond of cornflower blue[29], or open squares, or mayors. Instead they liked narrow passageways. They were people of the passageways. They were crowd people. They were the kind of traders who would sell you the wind. They tired of stealing from pockets and trousers, and instead whipped the hats from peoples' heads. Then someone who was in the crowd would suddenly realise that his head was cold, that his hair was stirring in the wind, and he would reach with both hands for his hat.

And the hat had gone.

Then he shouted 'Thief!'

And everyone began to shout 'Thief!'

Then, slowly, a blue kaftan with a green top shirt would appear. He wore a blue cap and a blue cape, and a sword with a brass scabbard. He had come to catch thieves. And he would catch the thief, if he came upon him, and then everyone would wait to see what would happen and if other cornflower blue kaftans would come up to help. If they did he would be seized and laid face downwards with his hands tied behind his back, and he would be flogged on the back with a navy cat of nine tails.

But, actually, they were in no hurry, the blue breeches, the blue caps. They did not hurry to catch those thieves, to come quickly up to give help, succour. That was not in their nature. As they say in the comic play "I do not delay, I proceed, I bring a charge, of course." Yet he continues standing on the spot.

But now the mud was warm, and the meat in the meat and skin stalls was getting darker and floppy – spring was coming. The craftspeople kept an eye on things, and because it was hot they looked out the things which were not the most needed, but lightweight things which

[29]   *Police uniform*

they had long intended to buy and had then forgotten all about. They traded a long time, and then bought of a sudden, only to regret it later. They mostly traded in metal goods, sewing haberdashery and leathers.

There were few beggars in the new city. They did not come there. They were put off by the fact that in Petersburk the earth was sweating and drove up mists. The large-scale beggars stayed in Moscow. But when the air became lighter they came in small groups, and here in the tartar settlement were the small-time beggars. Some were staying with an uncle or an aunt or came up for a short while from their home estate, or went to ground here in Petersburk. In winter they sat tight and came out as spring arrived. They slept a little in the first part of the day, then got up and changed families, and time weighed heavy on them, because there was so much of it. One hour passed and then another, and still nothing and no one – and still a long time to go before food. And this brought on melancholy. Then all at once they would rush to the Tatar settlement to look at various items, or to ask the price, or have a tooth pulled at the tooth tent, if they had a sore tooth. To breathe in the spring air at the scent row, or in the fish row, or to rummage in the old clothes, or in the rows selling hats or gold goods.

The three 'blind' old men passed through. They were given an onion each. Beggary wept and sang along the walls, and Ivan Zhuzla aka Ivan Zhmakin passed through with his light tread. He did not deal with anyone, pushed and shoved no one, and said nothing. He just observed everyone, and his look was not lofty or mean – but average, in the middle. He looked at peoples'hands and what they were holding, and only then did he look at their face. So he saw hands and arms in demi-uniform sleeves; in sackcloth, and above the sackcloth red uniform cuffs, and he chuckled. And in one pair of hands was a ball of wax, and Ivan took a step forward and gave a nod and a wink to one side to one of his people. Then he asked the price of the wax, worked it in his hands and rolled it into a ball. The ball was strong and did not yield, and he looked the deserter soldier from the Balk regiment in the face. He asked about this and that, and then took him to one side. He called the soldier a grenadier, and the former soldier of the Balk regiment puffed out his chest. Then he took him off to the tavern to have a drink on the deal, past the very nose of the quarter-master general of the police command – he of the blue cap, and Ivan even winked at him.

In the tavern the soldier of the Balk regiment spent some time downing drinks with Ivan, and became animated, and started talking about music and the military units. About how he had served in the cavalry, about how he had not done any bombardier training, and why not, and about how he was now a guard, and there were three others with him, and a Swedish dog, and about how he was not afraid of anyone, and how he would go on guard alone this very moment if asked, and how the other three would go walking round the streets, that he was a soldier of the Balk regiment, that's who he was.

"A Swedish dog? That's rich!" Said Ivanko, " Tell me, grenadier, what's the name of this Swedish dog? Was his owner a Swede who died at the battle of Poltava? Most likely."

"The dog is called Hunsfott, but where Poltava is, I don't know," said the soldier of the Balk regiment," Nobody ever told me."

But at this Ivanko gave a bored glance at the soldier, and placed the wax ball back in his hand, saying that this wax was not suitable for mould casting, and so he did not want to buy it, and so he drifted away, soft step after soft step.

* * *

That night he began to grow noisy, tearing his clothes, and summoning the whole household, with dog whistles, a great deal of singing, shooting at the wall-hangings and the ceilings, at the same panel where there was a sketch of the actor that looked like him. The actor's belly was shot through, and other parts.

And on the following day there emerged from the Yaguzhinsky house, from that same Yaguzhinsky 'chandelier', a team but not a team, a suite yet not a suite – a group of people with guns, whistling and singing. There may have been up to twenty of them.

And at their head walked Pavel Ivanovich, Yaguzhinsky, wearing his star, his ribbon and his sword. He was unsteady on his feet. Passers-by fled from them in panic, others turned their horses aside, and the street and turnpike guards ran away from them, and the sergeants and quartermaster sergeants of the police command, stood to attention with their mouths gaping open.

And in Yaguzhinsky's suite was the noisy Swede Gustafson, and he was playing on the piccolo, with passion, with all his might. Others, as they progressed along the Nevsky prospect road, shot at birds, since the ducks on the marsh had already flown in. Shooting them was forbidden by ukaz, yet many wild birds were killed, and two bullets hit a cottage. As this happened the gentlemen of the suite passed water on the ground and shouted out various obscene words.

And this suite, with its leader, passed along the streets, like a flood or a hurricane which is called a tornado.

On its way the group burst into discordant singing. They all sang together, like a choir:

"Passion and incense

Brought love, love!"

And then one hoarse voice bawled out:

"Stop your flattery

And all tempting.

You in no way comfort me!"

And then in chorus they all roared out:

"Passion and incense!"

And although it was a love song, when accompanied by frenzied shrieks on the piccolo and the constant bawling and sighing it sounded vaguely threatening.

And no one could later recall how the whole suite, or to put it differently the whole command or company, reached the river and crossed it and made its way right to the Kikin house.

And at the head of them all there hurried, borne by the wind from behind, wearing his star, cavalry and sword, and banging down with his hand a heavy staff or club – the Procurator-General himself, and his face was heavy.

And, before either the guard, an ex-soldier, and the other freak could work out what was happening, into the Anatomy house, the Kunstkammer, there streamed the whole company, the whole command. Yet once inside they lost courage, because, calmly looking at them, were the drowned babies, the frogs, and the smiling boy the structure of whose brain and skull could clearly be seen. This was Science. And they halted in the entrance chamber, where the guards stood, looking on and trembling lest there be any spoiling, breaking or stealing of the exhibits, lest anyone should walk off with one of the jars, or one of the birds in their pocket. Also standing there were the two-fingered ones, looking with human eyes at these noisy people, but they were idiots, and also quiet. Balthasar Shtal' stepped forward, and said in a hoarse and quavering voice:

"I am an apothecary."

But, without looking at him, the Procurator General walked on. He was followed by only two of his suite, the Swede, Gustafson, and one other. Six-fingered Yakov followed them. He walked behind the Procurator-General, his head stretched forward like a hunting dog that catches the scent of game, and is obedient and contained within himself. Because a live bird had flown into the Kunstkammer. It was a wild bird from the streets, plump and with blue silk plumage, with a star, and carrying a sword, and it was a man, and he was not walking but flying. In the chamber where there were various Siberian gods with fake musical pipes one other person had come to a stop. And into the portrait room came that same fat bird with unseeing filmy blue eyes, and then in came two people: the Swedish man, Gustafson, and the freak with six fingers, Yakov.

And, flying into the portrait room, Yaguzhinsky stopped, staggered, and suddenly turned yellow. He took off his hat and stepped nearer.

Then there was a whirring and squeaking, like a clock gives just

before striking. The waxwork stood up, inclining its head slightly, making a kindly gesture in Yaguzhinsky's direction. It seemed to be saying:

"Greetings!"

This the Procurator General had not expected. He was discountenanced, gave a hesitant bow, and took a step to the left. Then the waxwork turned on its long weak legs, which had been so long sitting they had withered. The head tilted back and the arm stretched out, and pointed at the door:

"Get out!"

Yaguzhinsky understood the anger, but he had been his aide de camp, and knew how to assuage this anger. One thing he had realised from the start was that the anger passed over and ended as a result of seeing a pretty face, but there were no women here, only a reindeer, and other boring things. And, making a gesture which he knew the other man liked, he put his hand to his breast, and began to try to persuade him that he, Pashka, Pavel Ivanovich, had no one else to go to, and that was why he had come to see him, just to have a quiet talk for a while and to have a look, and that he should not drive him away, that he was right now in a rumbustious mood, and had been for two days, and it was not his fault. And, as he said this, he crept step by step nearer the middle of the room, and then the arm fell back down.

And Pavel Ivanovich began to talk, and he began to complain while the Swede, Gustafson, stood by, self-important and drunk, under-standing nothing, while the freak listened, understanding every word, while the speaker talked more and more, and in the end was already shouting, as the waxwork stood, inclining its head.

"It really wasn't me, but him! The instigator of all whoredom! And his skill is to deceive people, every last one, and rob them. He drops the crown and kisses her hand – 'Majesty!' – while he himself marries and divorces, has his eyes set upon kingship. And he takes from others and brings it to the crown. And they are already closeted together, just the two of them, day and night. He has summoned the boyars - thief! He refers to your written instructions as 'dead'. He threatened me with arrest and was going to draw his sword. I've never in all my life seen anyone above like that!"

And he wept, the tears running from his blue eyes, like pitch, and he was wiping his nose and sobbing at his plight, bent double with self-pity. He shouted with all the power of his Yaguzhinsky throat:

"And who is the natural father of this son from hell?! A stable boy!"

And the waxwork inclined its head of Peter's coarse, wiry hair and listened to Yaguzhinsky. And Yaguzhinsky stepped back. Then the waxwork also fell back in the chair with a bump, head tilted back, arms hanging limply. Yakov, the six fingered one, stepped forward and placed the arms back on the arm-rests.

And then, making an effort and looking wildly around, the drunk and weighty man, who had flown in like a bird, stepped back and caught sight of the Swede, Gustafson, and was amazed. He turned sideways and caught sight of Eois, the dog.

And, still not taking in what was happening, he reached out his hand, stepped forward, and stroked the dog. And so he left, now much subdued.

A rumour went round amongst those in high positions. Few people of the middle rank understood it. They were busy with their own affairs, and it did not reach them. Amongst the lower classes there was little rumour, or if there was very rarely. Amongst the cavalry and those with ribbons there was a widespread, noisy rumour. It was seen by all and heard by all. The Swede, Gustafson, did not understand Russian and so was not affected by it all, and had grown accustomed to it, besides his only task was to play music. He got his board in the Yaguzhinsky household for his music – vinegar, firewood, candles and bed. The guards in the Kunstkammer were there to look after things in case anyone dropped one of the babies, or the monkeys in jars, and for them this was a rumpus amongst their betters, something to do with the spring maybe. They never went to the portrait room. There remained Yakov, the six-fingered one. His sense of the rumour was at the moment like that of the lower orders, and stayed within him, like corked wine. He had watched and listened, and he had placed those arms back on the arm-rests.

When the Prince of Rome, after baring his sword, arrived home red-faced, his blood stirred up, he did not know what to do. If Peter had been alive still he would have driven straight to him, fallen on his knees, and given that look, languid and sidelong, which he knew the other would in the end be unable to resist. And he would have put him, Pashka, on the block, and then, maybe, he would have forgiven him. But now? But now there was complete freedom to put him on the block, lock stock and barrel and to clear out his house, the disorderly tavern. But that would be too free-handed, and somehow he did not want to. If things were too open it was not a reliable business. He knew that from battles. He did not want to go to Marta, or to Katerina, and he went home.

He felt the cold and his blood had become tired. He had become stooped with age. He kept his winter coat on, and hid his nose in the collar.

And then, when Minister Volkov reported about the Kunstkammer, he went to the Kunstkammer. In his high-collared fox furs, the collar was lamellar, sable, covering his nose, off he galloped. And when this nose poked out, pointed as a hatchet, from the furs, it became so quiet it showed that only the reindeer was breathing, and that only a little, and perhaps the monkey in a jar, but the people had long stopped breathing altogether.

And at this point Balthasar Shtal', the assistant, stepped forward and said in a faltering voice,

"Highness. I am here an apothecary..."

But he did not look at him, and said nothing to the German.

And, turning his nose to the two-fingered ones, he saw that they were fools.

In an even voice he began to question the guards. The guards answered and heard the reindeer's heart beating. Then, when he had listened to the guards, he thrust out his arm in a well practised manner, and took hold of Yakov by the scruff of the neck. And Yakov felt he was propelled easily, as though walking on air and in the direction that he was steered.

And he led the way into the second chamber and there the grip holding the back of his neck was relaxed, and the six-fingered one came to a stop like a pendulum that had been stopped.

And, without looking at him, the fur collar went on questioning him in a calm voice. Then, in a twinkling, Yakov became cunning and decided that he would not repeat what he had heard at all, but that he would say that he had not heard anything, and at once decided to say little and make things up. And the next moment the fur collar looked at him with human eyes full of boredom, like coals when they are burning down, and the six-fingered one heard himself relating everything that he had heard and seen, and was amazed to find that he had remembered things he had not heard at all. Then the fox-fur coat gathered itself together and the bored eyes looked once more at Yakov's head, at his eyes and at the six-fingered hands – then at the slant-eyed baby that was there in a jar – and then moved off quickly, made a noise going into the portrait room, and then the door closed behind the coat.

And then Yakov, still standing where he had stood, quickly poked his head towards the door, and looked through the keyhole. The coat was standing there like a brick wall. And the wall moved, slowly shaking, towards the waxwork, the likeness.

And then the six-fingered one saw a hesitation, saw the waxwork stand up, and saw from the side how the finger pointed –'Go!' Yakov managed to take a step backwards – for straight at him through the doorway ran a man in a fiery crimson kaftan, and he was slim and the fat fox fur-coat ran after him like a live animal. And he bumped into Yakov, the six-fingered one.

There the two men looked each other in the eye. The fur coat went past, sable collar raised, nose hidden. He knocked over as he passed a Chinese god or a Siberian idol which rolled about. The guards rushed forward to pick it up. The man did not turn round, and then straight as an arrow he disappeared somewhere.

And they all clasped their hats and stayed where they were.

8

What a night followed!

Grey.

The weather had suddenly changed, a wind had got up, and everything was turn about. It was moving towards spring, and now you could expect cold or high water – 'middling weather', and there weren't the usual stars and moon in the sky. There was just the Milky Way which teemed with little stars, and the earth was dark, and the wind and the ice. It was harder to see than in the dark. This night was full of longing and anguish in Petersburk. It was hard for the boats in the Admiralty dock. They swayed and groaned at their hawsers.

It was quiet now in the Yaguzhinsky household, because the house was secluded and everyone had gone to bed; they were either half asleep or fully and deeply asleep. The Yaguzhinsky house was now like an island in a fairy-tale called the Mountain of Love, reached by no news, and surrounded by quiet water. Because nobody knew what was going to happen now, and where people would be sent. But that they would be sent away everybody was convinced. Fallen, blown past. Empty headed.

But the empty headed one was now sitting quietly, his drunkenness had subsided, and thought had returned. He still could not remember what the things were he had forgotten. The lamp outside the window was swaying as though drowning. Then he read his horoscope which an astrologer in Vienna had composed on the basis of the lines on his forehead. It had cost a fair amount and he had only limited reassurance from it.

According to this horoscope, according to the latitude of the planets, he was heated and humid. The common people loved him, but not noble and powerful persons. March indicates difficulty in his affairs because of spiteful persecution by political figures and members of the court, concerning his interests and gains. And it was now March, the very month. And he did have enemies on Vassilevsky Island, and political and court enemies – it was all true. However, Argon the storyteller also maintained that the above-mentioned enemies could not undertake any action, and that he would remain on top, and overcome all opposition.

And he also recalled again, without the help of any horoscope, a Viennese noblewoman, and this made him happy because he was not only her lover, but she loved him. She was smooth-skinned, dark browed, but had unfaithful eyes and sulky lips. And that smooth, proud noblewoman was in Vienna while he was in St Petersburk, and they were both, as though by a cord, drawn to each other by all the geography – and this was the state alliance with Vienna, which was necessary and useful for all. He could not live without her. And people did not understand this. And what? Enough! It could not be.

And this year, said the stargazer, Saturn passes the end of Mercury. Mortal hatred of the minister and his guile. Unkindness of highly placed persons. Interference. And victory. And life would open out with good fortune for up to fifty years or longer.

Yet all this was nonsense, and he had spent money for nothing.

And the Viennese noblewoman was far away. What was she doing now? She was either engaged in pleasant chatter or lying ill. But what would happen to him tomorrow – this the horoscope did not know.

He went over to the window, and saw- tin roofs, branches, mud, smoky air, and noise as though someone was pottering about down below.

And it seemed to him that his first wife – insane, a fool, had escaped, fled from the monastery and, hitching up her skirts was galloping round the house putting him to shame.

Then he looked out again and saw: branches, mud, old rags, a grubby statue of Flora, carrying something in a bowl. He gestured dismissively and stepped back from the window.

In the Vyborg wax yards it was also night, a manufactory night.

The workshop stood locked up – and all the cottages as well, the hut with the money and the shed with a stove. In the courtyard were two wagons. The soldier of the Balk regiment was wandering about behind the shed when he heard low voices, and he called the Swedish dog.

"Hunsfott!"

But the dog did not bark. The soldier of the Balk regiment sat down on a bench, closed his eyes and dozed. Then he called the dog again, and again it did not appear. He went over to the cottage where the money was and heard something, a scraping noise of metal on metal. He gave a shout, but there was no answer. Suddenly there was the noise of running feet, someone thumped him on the head and a voice said:

"Hey, grenadier!"

 - and then he slid to the ground.

When he came to he saw a tin roof, branches, factory night, and the door into the shed stood open. Then he whirled with his rattle, realising there had been a robbery.

And on Vassilevsky Island was the Menshikov house, and a Menshikov night. In a highly heated room he was sitting there warming his feet in their shoe socks in front of the fireplace which was tiled and blue and built about the same time as Peter's. He looked into the burning coals which were fitfully glowing and at the parquet floor on which the glow of the fire was playing like a kitten. He was smoking his long pipe, and letting the smoke out in big puffs. He was thinking that he had grown old over this past year, yet was not descending into old age, and he also thought the old pain had reoccurred in his legs – scurvy – which Dr Bydlo had treated twice, but not cured. And that in the summer he would be going to Oranienbaum for a rest and to put his house in order. He would thin out the big vegetable garden and install some kind of grotto with fountains and flowing water, or he would put in the pleasure garden marble walkways with statues and vases, and on the terrace he would put that new game of driving balls through hoops with mallets – malbanque – the dovecote he would have decorated by an artist. This new game was very amusing, and was full of argument and chance.

He would rest. Let everything in Oranienbaum be luxurious, and he would take with him a toy bodyguard of young boys, like the sultan the ambassadors had told him about. He gave a chuckle and puffed at his pipe. And he would sow some flowers. He liked flowers. He would crush them in his hands and sniff them. And he did not need anything, only to get away from his great losses and the great insults he had to bear before time. And from whom? From a scatter-brain, a common man from the streets. He would rest in Oranienbaum and summon her to him, and if she would play that game – malbanque. And he would marry off Marya to one of Peter's sons. Only then would he get back on his feet. Then he would sing 'Ai! Svat lyuli!'[30] to Pashka. It was about time Pashka stopped lying about him: 'the bream is a passing fish.' Pashka would well sing about bream – on the scaffold. Now he would be sent to the Samoyeds[31] in Siberia. Just let her come to Oranienbaum. She would drink wine until she shook and fell over, and she would play tricks and fool around. And his health was the main thing – you could not do without health! But his health was getting worse. Oh,Bydlo! Bydlo!

Then he asked for Volkov to be called, and he said to him:

"About the Kunstkammer business: the freak, the six-fingered one. Keeping this freak, the six-fingered one in the Anatomy House is not a good policy. He's quick-witted, and will repeat what Yaguzhinsky was yapping about. I hesitate to arrest him because there are the exhibits, and all the foreign embassies know about them. I don't expect him to alter his story. I should put this six-fingered one in a jar with double spirit; put him in spirit. But there aren't any jars big enough for this. Put his hands and feet in two jars. In double wine

---

[30]   Hey nonny no!
[31]   Natives

or in spirit, as available. But it should be done quietly. Go tomorrow and take him some wine from me, and to go with this gentle wine take this apothecary's box."

And he smiled "so that he enjoys it."

Chapter Six

*"I want to pour oil on the fire
and inflame your ready wit even more"*

PASTOR GLÜCK

The night came to an end, colour appeared in the sky, a faint pink. No one had yet risen, and the cottages, the stores and the manufactory yards, and the palaces and the canals were still deserted and dead. Then, in the cottages and the palaces the floors shook from a rumbling, and the window panes shuddered and shook slightly. And that was the first salvo, as though a dog of great size was growling, like the Neva River, but was still not barking. Those who were asleep shifted in their beds, and the first salvo did not wake everyone, and along the river, through the bogs and the groves there boomed a second salvo, and this was already a bark.

Then everyone woke up.

Half dressed, still in their underclothes, the maids came running out into the courtyards, and stared into the distance: what is it?

The upper class people clapped their hands, and the servants stiffened in their lowly quarters: who is it?

Then there was another salvo – a prolonged one.

And with it the city was on its feet.

Prince Izhorsky hurried to the window and looked out sternly, and when the ground shook from the fifth salvo three thoughts had already gone through his head. The first thought was a sleepy one – that it was the Swedes. But he rejected that because what would the Swedes be doing attacking now when Charles was in his grave and there was a treaty with Sweden? It was a half awake idea.

The second idea was that it was Pashka – Yaguzhinsky. He got up to mischief and fired off cannons. But he rejected this idea even more quickly. For a start, he couldn't get hold of any cannons, and secondly, he would not be bothered to do it.

The third idea was - a flood. The sea had got into the city and would drown all their goods and belongings. But then some wagons galloped past the window, and in them were soldiers of his lifeguards regiment. And the horses were as though half-crazed. They were almost slipping to their knees, while the soldiers were lashing them with three-tailed whips, and canvas was sticking out of the wagons on all sides, and as they rounded corners the wind took the canvas. And this canvas was sails.

Then he opened the window and commandingly waved to them to stop:

"Where are you going?"

But the men could not stop as the horses were dashing headlong, eating up the ground. You cannot stop boats like this either, and the horses were breathing heavily with the effort. From the wagons came the fleeting answer:

"To the Vyborg side!"

And he realised there was a big fire. He looked at the sky, and the sky was red.

There was a great deal of rushing and running. The gates of the barracks burst open and out flew the soldiers dragging long water hoses like snakes. The bell ringer brought out his bell and began ringing it. He sounded the alarm.

They brought out the chains with hooks on and that caused a rattling chain noise, the noise of the torture chamber – these hooks were put onto carts. And the church deacon who had lived snugly in his cottage for these past three years, and had made a vow not to shave or cut his hair, and just growled out his words in a deep voice, this deacon now leapt out with a white dove beneath his sackcloth. Because the time of miracles had come he had to throw this dove into the flames and the flames would die down. He had kept this dove in readiness for two years already. And he walked off proudly, the hair on his head matted, hatless, with the dove scratching at his chest.

Great shields of felt and big sails were put up by the Liteiniy, where the arsenal was, and if that went up in the air then it would restore the old tsardom, since the new, and the new city and all the colleges and bathhouses, and monuments, would go with it.

And Ivanko Zhmakin put in an appearance. With a light, prancing step he made towards the fire. He had anyhow not slept that night, and now he was running towards the fire. And the firemen were running, dragging out of the way anything that came to hand, clothing, gold, or they maybe came across whole fireplaces, or good pieces of canvas. And Yaguzhinsky rode out on horseback, Procurator General, crying out:

"Hey! Where to?"

And no one knew where the fire was. If the fire was on Vassilevsky Island then the hoses needed to be dragged out without delay, and straightway needed to be placed in the ponds – time costs lives. Because on Vassilevsky Island special ponds had been dug out to facilitate pouring and extinguishing. And if the fire was on Admiralty Island, then covering the dockyard with sheets, and using the sails to keep off the wind was one defence. Then everything alight was dragged out, whatever it was, because the Imperial Fleet was in danger.

But there was no fire there, and people began to ask where the fire was. The fire was in the Liteiniy area. And the artillery is the main department of the state. And if the artillery explodes that is final for the city and for everything else. Then all the wagons galloped to the Liteiniy.

And the fire was already drawing near the Liteiniy yard, and some of the cottages were already alight. The fire was already making for the bomb store.

So they shouted to each other, the bold ones went on ahead and the cowards dropped back, and there were lots of both the first kind and the other.

Carriages appeared on the streets, but without coats of arms on the doors. The foreigners were leaving the city because they thought the kalmuks were coming, that the kalmuk khan had taken the city.

They had left quietly, hiding their faces in their Russian bearskin coats. And they looked about them with foreign pride and fear. Their cash was in strong boxes. And the lowest beggars fled the city in heavy carts. They fled without anything, just saving their own skins.

Count Rastrelli woke after he had turned his hour glass nine times, and eventually broken it. Then he grabbed his latest piece of work and fled out onto the street, without his hat. And his work was not battles, and not some kind of brass bust of someone noble. He had just been casting in bronze the little figure of an arab. The little arab was pot-bellied, with laughing cheeks and a large navel. He had cast him as a test piece to check the bronze, and the evening before he had asked Legendre to fetch it over from the moulding shed, and when he had looked it over he decided he would add to the bronze the portrait of some noble woman, at its feet, because women in the city liked arab children, and the little figure would hint at the fact that beneath its robe it was bare, and that would be a source of amusement.

And now this morning he thrust the little figure under his arm and leapt out onto the street.

And the little wax horseman – the maquette for the casing in bronze, and for eternal fame, was left in the house and might , at the time of such a big fire, be stolen or trampled upon – or simply melt.

All around was very hell, but not like the one, already cracking open, with people enmeshed by serpents, which Michelangelo depicted in the chapel, but another, different, Russian hell, composed of horses' muzzles, children, soldiers, and ships' sails on dry land.

The wagons stopped in the Liteiniy. The old, patched sails had been hoisted in front of the Liteiniy yard to defeat the wind, and they were billowing out. It was as though another fleet was preparing to flee from the new Swedes. The wagons had come to a tangled stop, and could not go any further, but stood creaking from the strain. The colts were whinnying, and the mares were beginning to kick.

Rastrelli croaked out something or other, but nobody paid any attention to him, and then someone grasped him firmly from behind – and it was the trembling Legendre, his assistant.

The assistant was like a lost man, he was weeping, pleading to be let past, and shouting out that they were foreign artists – but no one was looking at him – and where to go Legendre knew not at all.

Count Rastrelli was growing a little angry. He was an outsider, a bird of passage – could hardly remember the original country of his birth, and did not want to return to his second home country. Strange times had come to these barbarians, and it was not clear to him what these sails were, why they were needed at all on dry land. Perhaps it was some kind of rebellion?

At that moment a horse bore down on him. The master took fright and thrust his fist into the horse's muzzle. The horse reared and looked sideways. Its muzzle expressed fear and incomprehension. The veins stood out, the mane was tangled. It was a young draught horse from the regiment. And then the master realised that he would put veins and nostrils like these on his monument, where the horseman would be placed.

"What are you shouting for?" he suddenly said to Legendre, "What are you crying for? You blockhead! It's just army and navy manoeuvres."

And he returned to his house, with the little arab figure.

In the Kunstkammer there was chaos. Balthasar Shtal', the assistant, had both hands to his head, and was standing in the main room like a Chinese idol. One of the two-fingered ones had dragged the reindeer out into the courtyard. The guards, dragging out some shields, were waving them about. The other two-fingered one had started to grumble and, croaking some incomprehensible words, took the jar with the baby and threw it out the window. The baby went flying out into the street, and finally, when they heard that the Liteiniy yard was alight, they dashed off, looking to save themselves.

Yakov had only just managed to get his shoes and his money-belt on, then he also rushed outdoors. He made his way after the guards, then dropped back. He looked around him. All around were soldiers, horses, grappling hooks and forks. Yakov quickly grabbed someone's mittens and pulled them on, but the soldiers standing on the wagon with their backs to him shouted:

"Pull!"

They were shouting about the fire hoses.

Now he was wearing mittens, and now he was no longer six-fingered, but five-fingered, like everyone else. And he gave a laugh and began to pull on one of the hoses.

But the fire was nowhere to be seen, and the houses were still standing. And suddenly water hit him, Yakov, and splashed the colt next to him all over the muzzle. It bared its teeth and squealed, as though it wanted to turn its head away and rush off.

Everyone began to run.

And when Yakov had run off a long way he saw that the sails had been lowered. And he heard how the wagons were singing. The pitch was smelling from the gentle movement, and the wagons floated off.

He looked at his feet – he had shoes on. He looked at his hands. They had mittens on. And he had got his belt. Then he strode off to the eating house, because he was hungry, and he asked the trader for kalach and a roll. Then he bought some goose patties, fish jowl, sourdough bread, and began to eat. He ate slowly and smacked his lips – and he ate thus for an hour or two, and then he finished off some calf's bladder, and then could eat no more. And when he was eating he did not take the mittens off, and the mittens became smooth with grease. He wiped his hands on his trousers, and knew that his belly was full, while his hands were full. Then he went off.

The alarms had fallen silent, and only a faint drumming signalled military activity. But in the city one woman in particular was laughing, and laughing until she could no longer stand up, and until she kicked her legs in the air. She stopped, and then it was as though someone had tickled her, and she collapsed again, unable to speak. And that woman was Yekaterina Alekseevna herself. The autocrat.

Because today was April the first she had thought up this joke to get everyone dashing about, and riding they knew not where, hither and thither.

Here she had fooled them all as was the custom in all the foreign countries amongst the upper classes to play tricks on the first of April.

It was already two months since the boss had died, and he had already been buried for two weeks. And the period of mourning was over.

And her laughter was so debilitating that they dosed her with water and gave her some Four Robbers smelling salts to sniff. And round about her all the maids of honour lay prostrate, to show how infectious her laughter was. And they were all half-dressed, almost nude, breasts bared, because they had not bothered to dress in the morning, and the evening was still a long way off. Many of them were even gently twitching their legs, and the forehead of one of them was heavily wrinkled as though she was in pain – such had been the effect of the laughter. But there had not been such great laughter amongst the maids of honour, because to begin with she herself had been frightened. And she did not laugh, but simply said:

"Ach! I've overstretched myself!"

2

And Yakov wandered round St Petersburg, and the canals made his head spin. He had never before seen such long, straight ditches.

He paid no attention to the metal objects along the Neva. He had already seen enough of them in the Kunstkammer. He went from place to place, the Admiralty Island and the Vassilevsky, and the Vyborgsky. He counted them all as settlements, villages, and between them were rivers, groves, bogs. At the Moika he pushed his way through the meat stalls, there he got stuck in the mud, and then he got frightened, not just at getting stuck, but that his sole would come off and everyone would see that he was six-toed.

He walked for a long while. He had money.

In the old clothes stalls on Vassilevsky Island he bought himself all new clothing, clean. A German barber gave him a shave. And Yakov began to look like a German craftsman of the middle rank in his leather mittens, clean shaven – it was obvious he was a German. To begin with he had walked round the edge of things, but now he began to walk everywhere. And some houses were roofed with withies, and some with shingles. On the outskirts, along the great Nevsky prospect road, there they were roofed with turf and birch-bark. There were few cattle. Only near the Letniy Island were there some milk cows, and beyond the clothing stalls by the Moika some sheep were bleating. There were no hives or pastures, and there was nowhere for them to be.

He still did not know where to settle, or how he was to earn his living. And so he arrived at the main island, the Peterburgsky, and saw the Peter and Paul church and the fortress.

On the church, in addition to the cross, there were three spires, and on these spires were some strips of canvas, long, narrow and coloured like snakes' tongues; a special church.

And at one house – a wide one – all one dwelling, there was an open space, and people were standing looking there. And he could hear the sound of human voices singing; and people told him it was a dance place. And for a long time he could not understand what that might be.

A man standing next to Yakov pointed out to him with his finger, and plucked at his sleeve without looking at him, and said: "Wow, look at him dancing around!" and the cognoscenti, the workers in the treasury looked on in silence, critically, with knowledge. A man was dancing about. In the open space stood the wooden likeness of a horse. Its neck was long – its flanks flat, legs and muzzle thin and small. Its back was sharp, and it was visible from above how thin it was, like a knife. And above it the very air was smooth. And round this monstrous horse stakes had been put in the ground, even, planed smooth, with pointed ends, a whole forest of them, like a pinewood. And the man was dancing on them. This man had no shoes on, was barefoot. He wore just a shirt. He was moving round the stakes on the butt ends. He would crouch down, nearly fall, and then clamber up again. And around the palisade stood armed soldiers, and the man ran up to the edge and fell on his knees, on the sharp pieces, and then with much howling and squealing he jumped to his feet and asked one of the soldiers something, but the latter pointed his gun at him, and the man went to dance once more. And Yakov moved closer. His neighbour said that this dance was an army and guard dance, as a punishment for guilty soldiers. Then the six-fingered one went even closer and watched them taking the man from the stakes. They did it awkwardly, gently, as people pick up children – and sat him on the horse. And he watched him holding on with his arms to that long wooden neck, and how those arms were gradually growing weaker.

And as his arms weakened the man sank down onto the sharp back and then howled and whined. Then one of the treasury workers told Yakov that the guilty soldier had to sit there for half an hour. And the woman selling kalaches told him that the soldier had stolen something or had something stolen, and so here he was, dancing, an she smiled, this kalach woman, and she was still young. And when those bare arms clasped the neck you could see how the human hand is constructed. What dips and hollows there are in it. He sat on the sharp spine, and then jumped up – and all around young urchins were laughing. That is why the place was called the dance square. Formerly the square had been known as the 'platz' square, and only when they began dancing on it did it become known as the dance square. A mother picked up her child and he watched the soldier and jigged up and down and gurgled.

"Why is he getting such a big beating?" asked Yakov.

"It isn't beating it's correction," said a treasury worker.

And another one added, "That's how they teach fools that nothing comes of nothing."

And when they took the soldier and placed him on some matting Yakov went up really close, and saw; lying and looking at him was Mihalko, his brother. The discharged soldier of the Balk regiment. Of the guard command. And his face was thin, his eyes had changed colour, and those eyes were wise.

And Yakov went past his brother as everyone was passing him, as time passes, or as you go past fire and water, as light passes through glass, as a dog passes an injured dog. At that moment he pretended not to see, that he had not noticed that dog, that he was a stranger who was going about his business.

And he went into an eating house, into a place where there were lots of people. Where there was steam, people and food.

3

He was sitting in front of the large mirrors, because today was the celebration of his birthday, and mourning had publicly and generally been stopped, and he wanted to dress in a fashion befitting his elevated status.

Today he wanted to be especially well-dressed. He was sitting quietly and directing a penetrating gaze at the mirror, a truly feminine gaze, not sparing himself, but searching out his good points. There was no beauty, but dignity and expansiveness in his bow and greetings. He undressed completely, and two servants massaged him with spirits from a flask. He looked in the mirror, and his skin was still young. They dressed him in a thin cotton nightshirt with full sleeves folded into thin pleats and lace cuffs four inches long, and his arms were lost in them.

Then they pulled on him some green Persian silk stockings, and, kneeling in front of him, straightened the gold buckles on his shoes.

And when they had put on his undershirt he sent away the servants, and left one, a barber. He himself arranged his neckerchief in three folds, and secured it with a pin with a crystal knot. And he straightened his new kaftan under the arms himself, and he fixed his own gold belt round the kaftan. Then the barber put his wig on, with its best French hair fluffed up, and then, looking in the mirror, he set his face – expectant with a slight smile.

He put on his rings.

He wore a red kaftan with a green lining, a green undershirt and breeches and green stockings. And with one hand he picked up his purse with the gold stitching – to pay the musicians, and in the other he held his feather muff of a scarlet colour.

These were his colours. They made him easily recognised at a distance by foreign dignitaries. And anyone who wanted to show him that they liked him or took his side, or party, put on red and green. And they were almost all dressed in the same style.

And he went to the palace and felt how much younger he was as a result of the spirit massage and the fine dress. He had laughter-playing round his mouth; it lacked only someone to joke with.

To begin with there would be a private conversation about finishing the Yaguzhinsky business once and for all – and then some fun with joking and some hot Hungarian liquer. And he would send straight to Pashka and arrest him and send him into exile.

And the breeze blew straight into his face – 'ai, svat lyuli!'

And once he had done with business he would supervise the making of a pyramid cascade in Oranienbaum.

Thus, in high spirits and with some joy, he drove to the palace, and went with a feather muff like a bird's plumage in his hands, around the rooms, and everyone bowed to the waist to him, and he saw who was wearing only a little silk on their back, or who wore some that was chafed at the sides, and thus he directed his bow to the autocrat herself. But when he directed his bow to her he saw that near to her stood Yaguzhinsky, Pasha.

And then Count Izhorsky started back slightly. Pashka whispered something and Yekaterina laughed and madame Lizavet put her hand to her stomach, such were the jokes he was telling her.

But Count Izhorsky only started back for one moment – he was a man of pomp, never lost his proud composure, and he gave a chuckle and stepped nearer.

At this Yekaterina stood up and took him by the hand, and madame Lizaveta grasped Pasha, led them together, and made them exchange kisses.

Pasha's kiss was cold, while the Count simply pursed his lips, and sniffed Pasha's neck with his nose.

'When had he been outmanoeuvred?'

And then, as quickly as he could, because he was a man of pride and a quick mover, he gave up the idea of sending Pasha to the Samoyeds or to Siberia, and he could still be sent with honour and no particular advantage, as ambassador to the Danish lands, or perhaps to somewhere less important, but at least far away.

And Count Izhorsky made a sign to the musicians with his hand, and tossed them a bag of money. At this the fagot began to growl like somebody's stomach, the fiddle began to squeak and the piccolo joined in.

And Count Izhorsky, Danilych, gave a laugh and crossed the room with his easy, bird-like, swaggering gate, which his wife was so fond of.

He half closed his eyes which clouded over, partly with pride and partly with hurt. And his eyes looked languorous, with a sense of injury, as though he had today begun to slip into old age. His eyes were exhausted. He went on to toss his rings to the musicians – and he was not sorry.

Then he sat down to play 'kings' at cards with Levenhold, Sapega, and Osterman. And he at once took all seven tricks and became king.

Osterman politely said to him – 'take' – and he looked at him haughtily and smiled, he began to find it amusing. He knew that he did not need to take, and that he should really say 'pawns'. But he was overcome by pride, laughter, and he regretted nothing, and so he picked up.

At this they all burst out laughing, and all that he had taken he gave to the others, and Osterman laughed so much that you could not hear him laughing, he had frozen. He was amused and carefree, and he had done this from pride.

And Yaguzhinsky, Pasha, was also happy. They called for him, begged him, and he knew what they wanted. He could tell amusing jokes. He was telling Yelizaveta about England, and that it was an island, and madame Elizabeth did not believe him, and thought he was making fun of her. Then he began telling her about the Pope's monks, and what strange sins they have amongst themselves, and everyone nearly died laughing. He got up to dance. And he threw the musicians some more money.

He danced.

There was to be no victory, and he realised that as he danced.

He would go home and go to bed. His wife was clever. She would calm him down. She was pock-marked.

And he, Pashka, would go to the city of Vienna, where his mistress was, the smooth-skinned one.

And, well, she would come to him and lie with him, and it would still not be right.

He realised that he had won, won everything, and yet the victory was not complete, and he could not understand why.

He danced the Kettentanz. The pistol dance which the boss had liked was no longer danced. And they danced with kisses exchanged with kerchiefs intertwined, in pairs, and the ladies had so much to drink that they made a tangle of all the dance moves, and they were dragged off amidst much gaiety, and many joined by kerchiefs reeled off into the next room where it was dark and warm.

Yaguzhinsky danced as well.

He did caprioles.

He had long ago abandoned his partner, and his eyes had clouded over. He could see nothing with them, but he went on dancing.

He was dancing because he did not know why this was not a complete victory. Why was it that he had won, and was possibly again in the ascendant, and yet there was no complete victory?

And he would see once again that Polish noblewoman from Vienna, with her unfaithful eyes, her full lips, and he would lie with her and that still was not everything.

And this was another matter altogether.

This was sheets of tin, branches, and his ex-wife had once again escaped from the monastery, the fool, and, hitching up her skirts, was there dancing round the house.

"Ai! Svat lyuli!"

And the guests were collapsing with laughter, all pointing their fingers at Yaguzhinsky dancing. Whirling and twisting he knocked the royal cook off his feet, trod on all the womens' dancing shoes, puffed out his lips – so carried away was Yaguzhinsky by the dance.

And he immersed himself in the dancing, and danced, and thus ended the day – 2nd April, 1725.

4

In the Kunstkammer two of the exhibits were missing: the head of a boy in a jar No. 70. The two-fingered one had thrown it out of the window, with the boy, on April Fools day, April 1st. His foolish eyes had made him pick it up and hurl it out. He had watched the others dragging out the reindeer and the Siberian idols, so he had chucked the boy out of the window.

And the six-fingered live curiosity, the freak, had gone. The two large jars of spirits which had been delivered to the Kunstkammer by order of higher authority, from the glassworks in Vyborg, were standing empty.

And the two-fingered ones had drunk the spirit from one jar, and topped it up again with water – and it had gone straight to their reason. They were in a state of high old good humour, and walked bumping into things, laughing and snorting, and they began to dance in front of the waxwork, and so clumsily that it stood up, and pointed at them with its finger – 'get out!'

And the idiots went off to their quarters, single-file, obediently. They were happy and carefree.

And the waxwork stood there, head thrown back, pointing at the door.

All around were his things – Peter's, the dog Tiran, the dog Lizeta, and the puppy Eois. Eois's fur stood up. The mare Lizeta that had carried the Hero at the battle of Poltava – with its horse blanket.

In the basement stood two heads, familiar, domestic: Marya

Danilovna and Vilim Ivanovich. And Marya Danilovna's right eyebrow was arched.

The Guinea parrot was hanging there, stuffed, with two pieces of dark glass for eyes.

It was just that the little grandson was not there. The brainless one had thrown it out the window, the important, golden exhibit.

And on a side cupboard was a great collection of minerals.

And all was peaceful, because it was great Science.

And Marya Danilovna's brow was still arched.

And in the Kikin House, in an official palace, was a waxwork, the work of a famous widely known craftsman – Count Rastrelli – who was now not far away, also on the Liteiniy, asleep.

But an important exhibit, a rare freak, a man with six fingers, had gone missing: this was a serious loss and an order was issued to catch him. At the time in question the six-fingered one was standing in a house belonging to a policeman's wife, Agaf'ya. This was a secret bootleg tavern near the unofficial trading bathhouse, and this and the tavern were open to some people, and closed to others.

And at this moment the six-fingered one was sitting chatting and opposite him sat Ivan Zhuzla, or Ivanko Truba, or Ivan Zhmakin, and both of them were sober.

"There is great Science there," the six-fingered one was saying, "great Science. There's a winged horse, and a snake with horns, and the whole lot is displayed just as it is, lying on cupboards. These cupboards are German work and made in the city of Stockholm itself. The fireplaces are clean. Some are shut away in cupboards to stop them being stolen – you cannot see them. And the other science is all in jars, wine jars. There is all kinds of wine – simple wine and double strength sharp wine."

And Ivan envied him

"They brought it from the German lands. The ship was Dutch, I remember.

But the most important science is in the basement, in jars – double strength, and that is a woman, and her right brow is arched, and no one in the anatomy house knows why the brow is arched."

Ivan looked sceptical.

"Why the right one?"

And then they gathered themselves together, and the six-fingered one settled up with the landlady. And as they were leaving one of the regulars warned them that they should look out for guards and turnpike keepers, because they were nearby, and it would be better to go straight home.

At this Ivan frowned, grabbed the tavern man by the scruff of the collar, and laughed.

And he said, screwing up his eyes, " If all the taverns had grain in them, then the whole city would be full of poor people. But now we are going down to the depths – to the bashkirs – to the nowhere lands."

And they went out.